DRIED FLOWERS
THE ART OF PRESERVING AND ARRANGING

First published 1972
Reprinted 1972
Reprinted 1973
Revised edition (in paperback) 1979

ISBN 0 7188 2386 9

Printed in Hong Kong

TO MY FATHER,

TO WHOM I OWE A CHILDHOOD LOVE OF,
AND LIVING ACQUAINTANCE WITH, ALL
GROWING THINGS, AND IN WHOSE WIDE
KNOWLEDGE I FOUND ENCOURAGEMENT TO
BROWSE AMONG HEDGEROW PLANTS AND
GARDEN LORE

CONTENTS

Part One

Part Two

Part Three

ACKNOWLEDGMENTS

IN ACKNOWLEDGING with warmest gratitude the many ways in which I have received most generous help from so many people, there are four people in particular to whom I should like to refer.

First of all, my thanks and appreciation are due to Mr Norman Puckering—invaluable and devoted gardener to the family for some thirty-five years. Due in no small measure to his dedicated labours and unfailing interest, the garden at the Manor House, Heslington, developed from a particularly uncompromising farm paddock into the present-day "dream garden"—which he has since tended so devotedly under the guidance of Mr George Smith.

Secondly, to Miss Dorothy Huxford—with us for some thirty-four exceptionally happy years, during which she managed to spare the time to assist with garden emergency chores such as hoeing, weeding, planting endless bulbs, dividing irises, picking plums (wasps and all), and watering—as well as much more. Then, as regards dried flower arranging, she became an expert in harvesting and assembling, and worked many long hours, for months on end, at superb arrangements, destined eventually for sale at our annual Red Cross boutique.

Thirdly, to Mr George Smith, who found time, in his busy flower-arranging life, to give me inspiration and guide-lines for writing, and much publicity, and who afforded me endless opportunities for collecting the favourite bits and pieces which are so essential for dried arrangements.

Finally, to my sister Susan my affectionate and deeply appreciative thanks are due, for her dedicated application and endless patience in typing and re-typing almost illegible manuscripts and adjusting incredibly bad spelling and erratic grammar. She managed to produce, at great effort to herself, a text without which this book could never have got launched, so to speak, from the slipway. She is now tackling this second one.

Then too, I should like to thank especially those kind friends who have allowed me to cull from their gardens, or who have brought me pickings from their travels. I am particularly grateful to Mrs Grace Blandy; Miss Lorna Carew; Mr Robert Day; Lord and Lady Derwent;

the late Lieutenant-Commander T. Dorrien-Smith, J.P.; Mrs Barbara Everard, F.L.S.; Lady Guise; Sir Ewan Macpherson-Grant, Bart.; Major Sir Rennie Maudslay, K.C.V.O.; Lord and Lady Mowbray and Stourton from whose garden at Marcus, Angus, I have had an invaluable range of greenery and, from Mr G. Mottram their head gardener, boxfuls of annuals which he has so carefully tended for me; the late Angela, Lady Middleton; the late Colonel and Mrs F. Renton; the late Major H. C. Ross-Skinner and Mrs Ross-Skinner; Mrs G. H. Smith; Mrs V. Spry; and Miss Eileen Warriner.

Numerous other people have helped me over the years, especially Mr E. L. Greenough, M.P.S.; Miss Odette Herbert; Lieutenant-Colonel W. D. Keown-Boyd, C.V.O., O.B.E.; Mr Stuart Kinch; Brigadier H. Leveson-Gower; Mrs Oliver Russell; Mr Alfred Simons, M.P.S.; Mr Graham S. Thomas, V.M.H.; and Mr Brian Withill. To them and to so many others I am deeply grateful.

I would like to express my warmest appreciation to Mr Russell Bennett for the trouble he has taken in his busy life to write the foreword to this book. Much of what he writes I fear is quite undeserved on my part.

Then, too, a very special mark of appreciation is due to Mr John Miller, to whom I am most sincerely grateful for the hours of detailed work he has devoted to his superb photographs of the arrangements. Figures 5, 6, 21, 22, 23 and 27 are all his work.

I should also like to thank Miss Jenny Overton and Mr Cedric Bush for their patience in steering me through the intricacies involved in the publishing of a first edition and the revising of a second.

*   *   *   *   *

My publishers and I are grateful to all who have generously given permission for the use of copyright material, and in particular: the Cambridge University Press, publishers of *1719 A Butler's Recipe Book*, edited by Philip James, in which appears the "Receipt for the Surrup of Long Life to be done in the Moone of May", by Dr Peter Dumoulin, quoted on page 148; Miss Roberta Chubb, the artist who drew the illustrated version of *Prayer for a Grandchild* which appears on page 146, and Mrs Nancy Smallwood, owner of the picture; Miss Alice Coats and her publishers, Adam and Charles Black, and McGraw-Hill, for permission to use material from *Flowers and their Histories* on pages 103 (the description of yarrow being originally taken from Marion Cran's *Joy of the Ground*, Jenkins, 1929), 114, 118, and 129; Miss Coats and Studio Vista Publishers for the quotation from *Garden Shrubs and their Histories* on page 121; Mr Peter Coats and Weidenfeld, George, and Nicolson Ltd for the quotation from *Flowers in History* on page 23, and the references on pages 108 and 130; Miss Margaret Rhodes, author of *Prayer for a Grandchild*, quoted on page 146, and the editor of *Country Life*, in which the poem originally appeared; the executors of the late Constance Spry, and J. M. Dent & Sons Ltd, for the quotations from her *Anthology*, on page 23, and from *How To Do The Flowers* on page 76; the executors of the late Hon. Victoria Sackville-West, and William Heinemann Ltd, for the quotations on pages 107 and 118; Miss Patience Strong and Frederick Muller Ltd for the extract from one of her *Quiet Corner* poems which appears on page 28.

LIST OF ILLUSTRATIONS

Colour Plates

11

AUTHOR'S NOTES

Introduction

An initial point to be borne in mind is that the dried arrangements mainly discussed in this book are on a fairly small scale—something in the range of twenty-six inches high by twenty-four inches wide, or less. Arrangements of this size are not cumbersome, and can therefore be moved fairly easily from one place to another. Within this apparently small scale lies an immense range of possibilities.

After a general Introduction, the chapters in Part I of this book follow a natural sequence through growing, harvesting, preserving and storing, to assembly. There are short additional chapters on containers and packing. Part II is devoted to the Florilegium—an anthology listing the plants which are of especial value, and which give particular delight, to the dried flower collector, with advice on how to harvest and preserve them, lightened with comments and quotations from the immensely long and rich lore of flowering plants, both in history and in legend. Part III begins with a short chapter, *Eyes and No Eyes*, about young people, followed by brief biographies of the herbalists who play a part in the Florilegium. The literature of flowers is, happily, a very full one, and listed in the Bibliography are several books which are of great value to anyone seeking to compile an anthology of this kind, and which point the way to fascinating records, contemporary comments, and early legends. A glossary of botanical terms, and a personal glossary of the flower-arranging terms used in this book (with some transatlantic equivalents), are also provided, together with a list of addresses which may, it is hoped, prove useful to anyone with an interest in dried flower arranging.

By Way of Making a Modest Start

Although the ensuing chapters attempt to describe an industry *par excellence*, in all its techniques and intricacies, there is no reason why beginnings should not be on modest lines. Leaves can be collected anywhere, everywhere, and at almost any time, placed between sheets of blotting paper and pressed under a sofa cushion, under light clothing in a drawer, or under the mattress of a bed not in use (pressing under the carpet would be unsatisfactory because high heels, electric sweepers, and the hard, non-porous nature of the floor itself would have a ruinous effect on such material as ferns, small sprays of evergreen, cypress, juniper, laurel, bramble and the like). A small beginning could well be made in drying seed-heads and grasses, either standing upright or hanging upside down—a shallow waste-paper basket or carton, a jug or plant pot would suffice in the first case, and a coat-hanger with a cross-bar in the second. The chemical preserving of flower-heads (that is, drying in crystals) would only involve a matter of a few days and the use of a small airtight box, tin, or (preferably) plastic container.

In the absence of vases or such-like containers for the arrangements, a small chipped sherry glass could be used; failing this, an ash-tray, a small tile, a patty tin, an ovenware dish or a paste pot would serve the purpose. A splendid base can be contrived with a small round of *stiff* cardboard, surmounted by neutral-toned Plasticine, which is in its turn covered with moss, lichen, cypress, abies, or box, in which the arrangement is set.

The Use of Latin Names

The use of Latin botanical names (much used in this book) is a controversial question; but how else would one end of the world know what the other was talking about? Many readers of gardening and flower-arranging literature tend to shrink from Latin names, and regard them as irksome, incomprehensible, and—apparently—wholly unnecessary: a form of snobbish cult. What, however, is a sure alternative? However charming and easy to remember vernacular names may be, they have a way of becoming confused and lost in the course of time—mainly, no doubt, because they vary not only from one country to another, but, indeed, from district to district. The complete stability of Latin nomenclature ensures a quicker and more reliable means of identifying the genus and the species, and when translated the Latin name often has a lasting and comprehensible charm of its own: *Astrantia*, for example, means "star-like"; and *Spiræa* conjures an image of Nausicaa and her maidens weaving flowery crowns, for it comes from an ancient Greek word meaning "a plant for garlands".

The botanical names used in this book are based on *Hortus Second*, by L. H. and Ethel Zoe Bailey.

The Language of Flowers

> *There's rosemary, that's for remembrance . . . and there is pansies, that's for thoughts.*
>
> William Shakespeare: *Hamlet*

The Language of Flowers, which also plays its part in the Florilegium, has changed very little over the years. Gabriele Tergit remarks in *Flowers Through The Ages* that the flower oracle game, played with a dandelion blowball or a daisy flowerhead, is as ancient as it is international

—"*Elle m'aime pas du tout, un peu, beaucoup, passionnement, à la folie.*" Symbolism and significance have gathered round the world's flowers, and become crystallised into a "language" of their own. The Greeks and Romans, for whom the natural world was informed with legend and myth, attached great significance to flowers, leaves and herbs, particularly in their religious rituals. There was a resurgence of interest in the Middle Ages, with the growth of chivalric customs and the importance of religious symbolism; and a revival in the eighteenth and nineteenth centuries. Some flowers have a common significance among the European countries: the pansy (which takes its name from the French *pensée*) for thought; the lily for purity and innocence; the laurel for glory; the rose for beauty. Gabriele Tergit describes how Goethe liked to send small dried tokens and flowery wreaths; once, she says, he sent an artichoke—knowing full well that, though only a thistle, it hides in its innermost centre what tastes best. A whole conversation could be created from the flower language quoted in the Florilegium; the difficulty is, of course, that with our spread-out flowering seasons, it would be a little awkward to conduct—unless, as described in the following pages, the correspondents had recourse to a well-filled store of dried flowers, pressed leaves, and seed-heads!

The Manor House, Heslington, York, where it all began

FOREWORD

by Russell Bennett

Studies serve for Delight, for Ornament, and for Ability. . . . Some Bookes are to be Tasted, Others to be Swallowed, and Some Few to be Chewed and Digested.

Francis Bacon: *Of Studies*

When I first met Nina de Yarburgh-Bateson, I was immediately aware (apart from her outward charm) of an inner feeling of tranquillity which she transmits. Seeing her surrounded by flowers in her sitting-room, made me feel that I was in a country house and that through the windows instead of a London skyline I should catch a glimpse of trees and meadows with an English country garden in the foreground.

It was only after our conversation was interrupted and I was left alone for a few moments that I realised that the bower of flowers around me, on side tables, pedestals, mantelpiece and shelves, were all preserved! Perfect in colour and shape, natural in outline, with curving stems and leaves, arranged carefully in varied shapes and subtle tones—but preserved! In fact, the only thing lacking (which sadly is lacking in many modern hybrids, anyway) was perfume, and this lack was amply compensated by the beauty of the arrangements.

My visit to Nina de Yarburgh-Bateson was instigated by reading the first edition of her book, now reissued in this revised edition. I wanted the readers of my magazine, *Flora*, to learn more about this talented artist, and hopefully, to learn some of the secrets of the (to me) magical way in which she is able to still the hand of time and to preserve flowers and plant material so perfectly.

I have found over the years since our first meeting, that her somewhat retiring air on first acquaintance masks a keen mind, unflagging vitality and bubbling sense of humour. Above all, she is dedicated to the art of preserving her flowers, and it is typical that she is constantly seeking to find new ways of using dried and preserved flowers—hence the new sections added to this book on Arrangements in Miniature and, more importantly, Arrangements in Churches.

Anyone who has seen the magnificent examples of her work displayed in the setting of St Peter's Church, Eaton Square, in London (two of these are shown in Figures 22 and 23) must realise the tremendous potential that there is for church flower groups to use this technique to beautify their own churches, particularly at times when fresh flowers (as is so often the case when gardens are empty) are too expensive to use in large quantities.

This book will teach the uninitiated, it will improve the technique of the experienced and will immediately broaden the knowledge of all flower arrangers and gardeners on the plants they should grow with drying and preserving in mind.

A love of plants was inherited by the author from her father, Alastair Macpherson-Grant. Summers spent among lovely Scottish scenery and winters in the New Forest meant that, as a child, she was always surrounded by nature at its most beautiful. She tells me that at the age of eight, she could list more than two hundred wild flowers from memory and, even then, she was busily pressing and recording them in a herbarium. Travelling extensively with her parents on holiday, exercising a talent for exquisite embroidery and lace-making and painting in water-colours (an aptitude which she has passed on to her daughter, Lady Mowbray and Stourton), all combined to give her a lively interest in design, colour and flowers.

Completing her studies at Bournemouth School of Art, she resolved to become a landscape gardener. Taking a diploma in horticulture at Reading University she went on to the University Research Gardens for six months' practical experience.

Her marriage to Stephen de Yarburgh-Bateson took place in 1929, and for the next eleven years they settled in Hertfordshire and she became a regular exhibitor at the Royal Horticultural Society's shows in Vincent Square, specialising particularly in alpine plants. She is a Life Member of the Alpine Society of Great Britain and also of the R.H.S.

When her husband succeeded to the title of Lord Deramore in 1943 he inherited among other estates Heslington Hall in Yorkshire (now the University of York). During the war years Lady Deramore became deeply involved in local community affairs as Director and President of the East Riding of Yorkshire Branch of the British Red Cross Society—work for which she was later awarded the O.B.E. (Civil).

At the end of the Second World War, Lord and Lady Deramore moved from Heslington Hall into the delightful Manor House on the estate which was a more manageable size for modern living. This was set in three acres or so of waste farmyards, buildings and meadows—what a golden opportunity for a landscape artist! And what golden results were achieved with the aid of donations of rare plants from gardening friends and expert advice on amassing a choice collection of shrub roses and clematis from Graham Stuart Thomas, V.M.H., the great rosarian.

Regular viewers of the B.B.C. television series "Gardener's World" cannot fail to have been enchanted by two visits which were made to the gardens of the Manor House, Heslington, under the guidance of the tenant George Smith, the internationally famous flower arranger. Obviously, changes have been made to some of the plantings since Lady Deramore moved to London on the death of her husband, but the restored eighteenth-century house, granary and walls, and her original inspiration, remain. Having walked through this garden in the early evening light, I can vouch for its peace and tranquillity, perfect sense of scale and proportion, and above all, its beauty both of flower and leaf.

It is this same feeling for colour and scale which Nina de Yarburgh-Bateson is still able to portray in her preserved flower arrangements.

Sadly Lady Deramore can no longer live in the home and garden she created (although it remains hers for life), but she does have the knowledge that her gardener, Norman Puckering, still tends her beloved flowers. He it was who had the task of harvesting and drying vast quantities of plants and shrubs when Nina de Yarburgh-Bateson first developed her interest in preserving flowers and arranging them.

As an idea to raise funds for the Red Cross, she assembled a limited number of dried flower arrangements and, with the added cachet of an opening by the famous Constance Spry, rapidly sold out and was besieged for more! From then on, the "dried flower boutique" became an annual event each autumn, and, through acting as a focal point for flower-arranging activities, eventually resulted in the formation of the York Flower Club.

On moving to a London flat, Lady Deramore thought that all these activities were behind her, disposed of all her dried treasures and (she thought) settled herself into an existence as a balcony gardener (yes, she has one). She had reckoned without her friends who, insistent that her art could be practised just as well in town as in the country, supplied her (and still do) with leaves and seed-heads for pressing and drying. Her local "barrow boy" and helpful florist are always kept busy furnishing her with roses, freesias, carnations and other seasonal flowers and some of the more exotic foliage which she uses and it is the results from these efforts which you see in the exquisite pictures throughout this book.

After reading it for the first time, I was inspired to try, in my own way, to create an arrangement of dried flowers. Since then, I have gone back, again and again, to its pages seeking help and advice on what to choose or "how to do it"—and I have never failed to find what I needed. I feel sure that every reader will find, as I have done, that Nina de Yarburgh-Bateson's practical advice is invaluable and her artistic guidance an inspiration.

RUSSELL BENNETT
Eden Park, Kent

Part One

To see a World in a Grain of Sand,

And a Heaven in a Wild Flower,

Hold Infinity in the palm of your hand,

And Eternity in an hour.

WILLIAM BLAKE: *Auguries of Innocence*

INTRODUCTION

He that has two cakes of bread, let him sell one of them for some flowers . . . for bread is food for the body, but flowers . . . are food for the soul.

Eastern Proverb

Gifts from Heaven

The dedicated collector of plant material for preserving can, like the great Linnaeus himself, "explore the recesses of Nature and cull the treasures of the moor, pasture and field—the river bank, and swamps," which, in due course with his own art, he can preserve and arrange, "to the delight and astonishment of kindred spirits". [1]

Anyone who seeks perfection, which is somewhat scarce in this world, should be prepared to forgive a plant for needing a measure of study and care. Any plant, he should remind himself, is a gift from Heaven, and no apology is called for in showing interest in its growing. As Constance Spry has said, this is "the accepted hobby of the learned and the great, the connoisseur and the beginner".

"Just before the light fades," as she wrote in an article quoted in her *Anthology*, "all colours seem to take on an added brilliance, and then, as darkness gathers, this goes, and new beauty is revealed in a world now full of gentler shades." It is worth planning to preserve this beauty, so that it does not vanish when the sun goes down nor shrivel when day is done. Here one can begin a new chapter in creative enchantment, and as each page is turned, so a new undreamed-of mystery is revealed, to fascinate the reader and to inspire him to explore further afield.

Arrangements With Dried Material

Would there were more lively, expressive words to describe an industry which offers such infinite possibilities to anyone with imagination and artistry to interpret its diversely exotic and yet simple charm; an industry open to all imbued with a love and feeling for growing things, and a wish to attempt to perpetuate them, so far as is possible (at least, in part), in their

---

[1] Coats, Peter, *Flowers in History*, Weidenfeld & Nicholson, p16.

own colours and forms, cultivated or wild, harvested at home or abroad; an industry whose materials are gathered in garden, woodland, pasture, field or hedgerow, whose aim is the picking, preserving, and arranging of flowers, buds, leaves, grasses, ferns, seed-heads, appeallingly fashioned fragments of wood, bark, or twig, and verdant moss.

It is not, alas, until the bleak months of winter arrive that the true wealth of summer vegetation comes vividly to mind. For those who long to conserve an all-the-year memory, a reminder of some favourite garden shrub or hedgerow flower—even a grass from a field— what happier idea could there be than to collect, preserve and assemble some of the harvest there for our gathering? But do not, please, begin gathering at the last moment, just as late autumn storms begin to take their toll; start during the months of warmth and sunshine, when plant forms and colours are at their best, neither burnt up by the sun, nor dishevelled by rain and wind.

Contrary to what is usually thought, many years and countless seasons of trial and error often pass before the techniques of growing, harvesting, preserving and, eventually, assembling dried material of all kinds can be achieved, to give the desired result. So much depends on climate and season in any particular region and in any given year, and their effect on the quality and quantity of the harvest. Those who are not wholly familiar with plant life in all its humours, its likes and dislikes, its varied characteristics, may feel that a certain mystique surrounds the ways of collecting, preserving, and indeed, of handling dried material; but in point of fact, anyone with a sense of adventure—a wish to experiment—together with time and much patience, can find the whole process as simple as it is absorbing, and ultimately enchanting. It is, moreover, a creative activity within the reach of anyone willing to succumb to its appeal.

Anyone handling dried flower arranging becomes more and more aware, in these days of pressures and inhibitions, of the truth of the saying "God helps those who help themselves." If there are no garden flowers, for instance, why not turn to the field, or the hedgerow? Why not create a supply of dried material to draw on when there is nothing fresh to hand, either to fill just a temporary gap, or perhaps for longer, to satisfy a need or even a whim? Of course one must say here, at the outset, that nothing—absolutely nothing—can equal colourful sprays of leaves and flowers growing in their natural surroundings, or freshly picked and arranged to delight us with their beauty and their fragrance for a little while. The flower arranger of today, professional or amateur, has raised his art to a superlatively high level, as is superbly demonstrated by Flower Clubs, up and down the country, at flower festivals, in cathedrals, in village churches, in stately homes, and similar places. His indeed is a true labour of love, an achievement giving beauty and pleasure to countless people, and benefit without measure to many charities. Long may their dedicated efforts flourish, and their theme-song "serendipity" prevail.

The main theme of this book, however, is the harvesting, preserving and arranging of all growing things, whether cultivated or wild, from florists', from markets or from street barrows, from one's own or from any other land. The dried sprays of leaves, flowers, seed-heads, grasses, ferns and lichens have a charm and delicacy all their own. They create their own characteristic atmosphere; they can mingle with all sorts and conditions; they can be moved from one place to another to enhance their surroundings with their muted tones; they can be dressed up or down, in colour, shape or style, and transformed in the light of a moment's inspiration. The final arrangement will be the due reward for those who have worked to fashion it. There are other blessings too: no water needs to be topped up or replenished; no vase needs to be cleaned; there are no dead flowers or leaves to be discarded; it is immaterial if a current of fresh air blows through or a cold draught creeps into the room. Work is saved and anguish spared, and maybe, pennies also, although preparation may have lasted over several months.

The ensuing chapters cover in detail the sequence in the processes here outlined: from fresh to dry; from cradle but not, definitely not, to the grave. Thanks to the techniques here described, there is no need for anyone with "a cold disliking eye" to regard anything dried as ghostly, lifeless or dead. Many years may pass before these dried plants, flowers and leaves join their erstwhile fresh counterparts on the gardener's compost heap. They can be invited to stay with us a little longer. So why not collect together even a few of our favourites from the treasures of summer months, and preserve them so that they will continue to enhance their surroundings, albeit in subdued tints, with their presence, and to keep alive in our midst the pleasure that they give.

GROWING

God Almightie first Planted a Garden. And indeed, it is the Purest of Humane pleasures.

Francis Bacon: *Of Gardens*

Introduction

First of all, growing for drying. The scope can be almost limitless and the choice tremendously variable, depending on soil, climate, seasons and prevailing circumstances. It is a subject as intriguing as it is absorbing and has unimaginable possibilities. It knows few boundaries as regards districts, countries or even hemispheres, and is essentially global in character. Who knows—one day the planets may provide the next hunting ground!

Ideally, the collector who possesses a garden, not necessarily a large one (and preferably with someone else to tend it), has an advantage, because the seasonal tasks of harvesting, preserving, and, to a large extent, assembling are, in themselves, all-exacting and time-absorbing, demanding constant and painstaking attention. There can be no doubt that a well-stocked garden full of trees, shrubs, climbers, herbaceous plants and bulbs provides the perfect source for drying and preserving requirements throughout the year, and with the addition of a green-house and conservatory it would indeed be a true answer to prayer.

Though the methods of garden and green-house culture, and how and where to grow, are outside the province of this book, there will invariably be a sensitive and inevitable link between grower and arranger—and the closer the better for all concerned. The main disadvantage for the former—if it really can be called a disadvantage—is that he may find himself somewhat short of ingredients for his precious compost heap!

Failing garden ownership, a collector who has access to friendly market gardens and private gardens in different parts of the country can find immense and positive help, without too many attendant worries. Alternatively, a collector who is mainly dependent on woodland, pasture, field or hedgerow, and—yes—railway banks, bomb-sites and waste land, will find an abundance of beautiful and exciting material, far beyond expectation.

Finally, material of all kinds can be acquired—fresh or preserved—from plant specialists, nurserymen or florists. Some of this material may be available at reduced cost, if it is surplus to sales requirements.

Before, however, concentrating on what to grow, consideration must be given to an item of importance: the affinity between growing and harvesting in the sequence of events.

The Affinity between Growing and Harvesting

In growing and harvesting, sowing and reaping, seeking out and collecting, there are so many worlds from which to choose, so many avenues to explore, so many fields from which to glean. For the dedicated collector with a perceiving eye, where there is a will there is also a way, even in the face of environmental or seasonal obstacles. If it is not possible to grow adequate supplies (and a gardener with a heart will never wish to over-prune) other sources for the precious materials will have to be found: the world of the wild, other lands, market stalls, garden centres, seed specialists' stocks. Furthermore, why not encourage others to develop a feeling for weeds? Even those who have little initially, may well in the end become imbued with the proverbial enthusiasm of the convert, to an extent which will surprise them. With a little ingenuity on all sides, no one need submit to the austerity of "grow or do without". Sources of supply may have to be reviewed from time to time, and new ones sought. Seasons, admittedly, will invariably be precarious, weeks unpredictable, days good and bad—but in the long run the diligent collector will survive, and his store may even one day boast a surplus.

A Further Affinity

There is a second point to be borne in mind. The true lovers of plants, whether they are growers, collectors, purchasers or arrangers, should share an innate understanding and appreciation of plants' respective needs. They will have a basic sense of value, form, texture, colour, shade and habit of growth, and an entente with nature, which will determine the way they use their material to depict the idea they have in mind. So far as the grower, harvester and arranger are concerned, there can be nothing further from the truth than to say, "*Le bon Dieu est toujours pour les grands bataillons.*"

Lovely as they are in their summer profusion, plants do not necessarily display their most beautiful forms or their most exquisite tints in the highlight of the year. Each week, each month, each season brings its own matchless character and loveliness. A bud, a leaf, a stem, a flower, a seed-head, a single grass, a fern, sedge, moss or lichen—all have their individual fascination and need not be displayed in great abundance to reveal their individual characters and evoke a lasting memory. A daisy or a rose, a catkin or a cone—bright in colour or muted in shade, cultivated or wild, in abundance or in short supply, they are all gifts to look upon with delight and gratitude, and to handle with sensitivity and care—and this applies to the grower, the harvester and the arranger of fresh and dried material alike.

By the same token, quantity or size are not of great account—it is quality that weighs, as Miss Strong has described:

> *God did not despise the doing of the tiny things—He must have spent a lot of time on making flowers and wings—He made the mountains and the seas, the whirling worlds on high—and yet He deigned to make the ant, the bee, the butterfly—the spider and the snowflake and the smallest bird that sings . . . the little things.*

The Principles of Growing and Harvesting

Growing and harvesting should proceed side by side throughout the year. Visualise, on the one hand, a well-established **evergreen shrub or tree** which is fairly common in this country. It should be possible for the collector to select leaves little and often (so long as they are mature), as and when required. With a younger, immature plant, on the other hand, or one of greater rarity, one must take into consideration its constitution and ultimate shape. Stress must here be laid on the importance of conservation. However keen the picker, and however desperate his need may seem, he must not, on any pretext whatever, be guilty of even a hint of vandalism or desecration. A plant is a precious gift of Nature, intended for all to enjoy.

With **deciduous shrubs and trees**, harvesting is a more seasonal affair and leaves are gathered progressively, as they become loose to the touch and almost ready to fall.

The growing and harvesting of **herbaceous, biennial and annual flowers and seed-heads** is again somewhat different, depending on the time of planting and the all-important weather conditions—both during the growing period and at the harvesting stage. In these cases harvesting should be timed with precision. A bloom picked a day too late may lose its colour and texture in the process of preservation, and a seed-head gathered when over-spent will wear forever a melancholy garb.

Much the same principles apply to the growing and harvesting of **grasses**, which must be picked before going to seed. **Ferns**, too, have their special seasons: their growing and harvesting may sometimes be extended over many weeks, as the fresh young fronds develop and the older ones mass themselves in tangled mats of spreading ground-cover. They need to be harvested in their prime—the fronds neither too young and over-supple, nor yet too strong and tough. The growing and gathering of **mosses** should run concurrently throughout the year, though this will, of course, depend on the weather—in a dry season one would pick earlier, whereas the opposite prevails in a time of excessive damp. Sunshine can enhance their highlights, while on dull weather days they contrive to show a specially green hue.

Growing and harvesting go hand in hand. Some seasons will be ideal, some diabolically frustrating, but there should not be many days—that is, fine weather days—when the collector, armed with his knife or secateurs, cannot find plenty of foliage, twigs, ferns,

Fig. 5: after infinite study of the superb Fabergé exhibition in the Victoria and Albert Museum, the desire to perpetuate the memory seemed a challenge worth facing. Here leaves and flowers are gilded, wired, and set in a small heading of Bostik. The vase stands on mirror glass, a string of tiny pearls surrounding its base, a similar circle of "diamonds" entwining its neck. *Thalictrum* leaves, be-jewelled *Ammobium* flowers and a sprig of fine *Briza* grass complete a shimmer of Fabergé.

mosses and lichen to stock his store. If growing plants are unavailable, either in the garden or in the countryside, the search can be extended to the markets, both in this country and indeed overseas—where the seasons may be different: the chrysanthemum may be with us in mid-summer, for instance, while the rose will present itself at Christmas. For the dried flower worker, such out-of-season trouvailles should be no problem. Anything can be preserved at any time, so long as the necessary system for preserving and storing is in readiness.

The main point to underline is that growing is practically inseparable from harvesting, and hence the chapters on these subjects are inevitably very closely related.

Useful Material To Grow and Gather

The following notes may be of help as a general guide, though fuller details will be found in the Florilegium in Part II.

TREES

Most of the conifers (that is, those with flat needles, as opposed to pine or spruce, which will not press) are useful, mainly for background work. The store should always contain as many sprays as possible of *Chamæcyparis* (False Cypress), *Cupressus* (Cypress), *Juniperus* (Juniper), *Taxus* (Yew) and *Thuja*. All these evergreens dry easily and retain their colour. If any of the gathered stems are especially thick, the small sprays can be removed from them and pressed separately. Pressed and kept in a cool atmosphere, they may well last for years.

Among the garden trees, perhaps the *Acers* (Maples), *A. Pseudoplatanus* (Sycamore) with its seed-head "keys", and *Sorbus Aucuparia* (Mountain Ash) provide the most beautiful and adaptable leaves for preserving. All these should be collected the moment they start to fall and should be placed immediately face-downwards between sheets of blotting paper for pressing. Some beautiful glowing maple leaves appear in Fig. 10 on page 45. Leaves of *Platanus acerifolia* (the London Plane Tree) together with its berries, are equally useful. The dangling seed-heads of *Betula pendula* (Silver Birch) are most graceful when varnished and invaluable in taller arrangements. So, too, are all varieties of eucalyptus—leaves and berries. Seed-heads of the common single lilac and sprays of young beech are also well worth collect-ing, and so too are the leaves of elm. The beautiful leaves of *Nothofagus procera* and *Parrotia persica* form charming additions to the collector's pressing store.

SHRUBS

The number of shrubs is legion. Luckily the policy of turning so many gardens over to flowering shrubs for economic reasons, is indeed a happy one for the collector. In this category the *Acer* (Maple) tribe again tops the list with *Acer palmatum* (the Japanese Maple) which has many varieties—*A. p. atropurpureum*, *A. p. dissectum*, and kindred varieties—all with flame-coloured delicate leaves which should be pressed and stored in blotting paper, with the greatest care (Fig. 25 on page 75). If sufficient quantities are available these leaves make exquisite arrangements set in Plasticine in candlesticks, with little else added. Many of the *Rosa* species have beautiful leaves, and the arranger should always be on the look-out for them. In particular, the leaves of the practically thornless *Rosa rubrifolia*, with their out-of-this-world soft grey-green colouring, and mauve-purple sheen are breathtaking in their delicate beauty. Among the other genera of the *Rosaceæ* family are many species which are worth the leaf collector's attention, such as the *Rubus* (Bramble) tribe, including the black-berry and kindred species, whether cultivated or wild.

Among the other shrubs with leaves useful for dried arrangements are camellia, rhododendron, *Aucuba japonica*, *Arbutus Unedo* (the Strawberry Tree) *Olearia Haastii* (the Daisy Tree) and *O. macrodonta*, *Prunus Lusitanica* (Portugal Laurel), *Laurus nobilis* (Sweet Bay), cotoneaster, *Siphonosmanthus Delavayi* syn. *Osmanthus Delavayi*—whole sprays of this should be picked for pressing (one appears in the centre of the frontispiece, behind the frontal helichrysum)—*Elæagnus ebbingei*, and hydrangeas, especially the *small* floret forms of *H. Hortensia* and the quite exquisite delicate blooms of *H. cinerea sterilis*—the correct time for harvesting these small creamy-white-green blooms is fully discussed on page 52, in the chapter on harvesting. *H. paniculata grandiflora* is also a "must" for the dried flower collector, with its white-shading-to-pink flower-heads, so invaluable for the basal front of an arrangement—either "inset" or projecting outwards, in all its beauty. (Beautiful dried hydrangeas are featured in Fig. 7 on page 37.) Other treasures are mahonia (leaves as well as seed-heads), laurel, *Rosa* species (many leaves press well), many of the viburnums, especially *V. Davidii*, and *V. rhytidophyllum*, and *Ruta graveolens* "Jackman's Blue" (Rue); *Rosmarinus* (Rosemary) also dries early in the season, when it can be lightly pressed. No arranger can afford to be without *Senecio laxifolium*—formerly *S. Greyii*—with its rather tough silvery-backed evergreen leaves. For high background sprays, the many forms of *Genista* (Broom) are useful. Skimmia is certainly worthy of inclusion here, both for its beautiful, dark, shining leaves and pretty berry heads, and so too are *Choisya ternata* (Mexican Orange), magnolia, *Pæonia suffruticosa* (Tree Pæony), *Pyrus salicifolia*, *Artemisia arborescens*, *Euonymus japonicus* and *E. radicans*, with its variegated leaf, and the quite exquisite *Gleditsia* (Honey-Locust). Among the half-hardy or tender shrubs which can be grown in green-house or orangery or bought on the market is the *Grevillea* genus in its different forms, especially *G. robusta* (known as the Australian Silky Oak)—this should be pressed in quantity and a good supply of it should always be kept in the store. Its fern-like leaf can either be used entire or broken up into short fronds for use in small arrangements and as background arrangement material, and it keeps for years. *G. asplenifolia* is quite different in form from *G. robusta*. Its long slender leaves with serrated edges and silver backs are most beautiful, together with its shining dark red arching stems and exquisite small red-brown flower-heads. It presses most easily and lasts for months or even years. It is quite invaluable to the dried flower arranger, and a supply of this too should always be kept in the store. Slender spears of *G. asplenifolia* appear in Fig. 8 on page 40.

The most useful climbing shrubs are found among the *Hedera* species (Ivies)—leaves and berries—*Vitis Coignetiæ, V. Henryana, V. vinifera purpurea* and *V. v. Brandt* (Grape-vines), and many of the clematis, especially *C. macropetala* and other species—clematis seed-heads, fluffy or varnished, are invaluable, and a few unopened varnished buds are pretty for a change. Both *Humulus scandens* (the cultivated perennial Hop), which can be grown as a climbing annual, and its wild counterpart, *H. Lupulus*, are attractive when dried for arrangements.

Furthermore, the dried flower arranger seeking flowers to preserve can choose from the wide, and immensely valuable, range of garden floribunda roses—particularly the commercially grown species such as "Garnette", "Carol", and others of the same kind, which can be readily bought at florists, in markets, and off street barrows. A number of small, glowing "Garnette" roses and softer, pink "Carol" roses, preserved by the chemical process which is described on pages 61–63, are shown in the arrangement in Fig. 10, on page 45.

HERBACEOUS PLANTS

With trees and shrubs the collector is mainly on the look-out for leaves, and in general only gathers a few seed-heads; the large category of herbaceous plants, both perennial and biennial, is his main seed-head source, though in some instances leaves and flowers or leaves and seed-heads are both to be found on one plant—acanthus and aquilegia, for example, or "Garnette" roses, or crocosmia. When collecting herbaceous material for drying, one depends mostly on picking from the border, and here there will inevitably be conflicting demands: the choice between cutting fresh flowers as they come into bloom, either for preserving or for fresh flower arrangement, or leaving them to form seed-heads for harvesting later. This decision can, at times, be more than frustrating! A typical example is the delphinium: so lovely when left to give colour to the border; delightful if picked while young and dried in the hot-air cupboard, to cheer the winter months: invaluable if one foregoes picking until its seed-heads are formed and ready for harvesting. *Molucella lævis* (Shell Flower) and *Ballota pseudodictamnus* are other examples, as are many of the charming and indispensable silver-leaved plants (pages 36–38). It may not be practicable to relegate part of the vegetable garden—if indeed it still exists—to "cutting" plants only, but where this is possible it does help to solve the problem.

The collector should keep an eye open from late spring onward throughout the year. For his harvesting he should grow such herbaceous plants as appear in the following list.

Acanthus, for its leaves and wonderful flower-heads (an arc of acanthus is drying in Fig. 19 on page 61; and there is also a description on page 101, in the Florilegium)

Achillea clypeolata, A. filipendulina, and the hybrids "Moonshine" and "Flowers of Sulphur", and *A. Ptarmica* with its varieties "Perry White" and "Pearl" (the genus is described on page 102)

Alstræmeria Ligtu hybrids, for useful seed-heads (the genus is described on page 105)

Anaphalis triplinervis, for its tufted flowers, indispensable for "insetting" in arrangements of all sizes (page 106 of the Florilegium)

Fig. 6: this arrangement, standing on an antique urn table, was designed to be used anywhere according to requirements. The white vase was filled, as usual, with Oasis covered with crumpled chicken wire, and these "mechanics" were covered with moss, attached with bent wire to keep it firm. A selection of dried red and yellow roses, in varying hues, is interspersed with small, much-curled, skeletonised magnolia leaves, with a backing of ferns, finely-leaved eucalyptus sprays and other varying green leaves: small pink larkspurs and red maple leaves add colour, and delicate white cycus grass introduces lightness (obtained from Handley Reed, whose address is given on page 154).

Anemone Pulsatilla (Pasque Flower)—and many others of this genus—for its invaluable delicate leaves (page 107 of the Florilegium)

Aquilegia, for its indispensable seed-heads—one can never have too many of these; the genus is described on page 107

Astilbe—in variety—for its plume-shaped seed-heads and good leaves

Astrantia (Masterwort), an unusual, attractive umbellifer described on page 109; its flowers make a most diaphanous addition to an arrangement, and should always be included in a dried collection; it will dry standing up in an empty container, or could be hung upside down in loose bunches; dried astrantia appears in Fig. 19 on page 65

Catananche cœrulea (Cupid's Dart)—the electric-blue and silver-backed daisy-like flowers of this delicate everlasting preserve well, and look lovely in small arrangements; they require careful handling when being processed (the treatment is described on pages 61-63 in the chapter on Preserving)

Celmisia, for its silver-backed foliage, featured in Fig. 26 on page 77

Centaurea Cyanus (Cornflower, Bachelor's Button)—and many of the wild knapweeds—will be good for drying, but the unopened buds, which should be cut quite early, are perhaps more important than the flowers and make charming light outline additions to a dried assembly; the genus is described on page 111

C. dealbata, for its beautiful seed-heads which glisten in the light and which are also very long-lasting

C. macrocephala, another hardy perennial, this time with a charming yellow flower-head which can be dried and which is much sought after for such arrangements

Crocosmia, for its magnificent seed-heads (page 113 of the Florilegium)

Delphinium, for flowers and seed-heads (page 114 of the Florilegium)

Dianthus (Carnation), for the medium-sized double pinks, their hardy hybrids and *Allwoodii*, such as the lovely "Doris" and similar types, which are absolutely indispensable. Though some flower more profusely than others, they come in a superb variety of colours and are described in detail, with coloured illustrations, in the *Pink and Silver Booklet* issued by Mrs Desmond Underwood (page 155). A drift of dried border pinks appears in Fig. 19 on page 65; and others feature in the centrepiece of the assembly on page 45.

Digitalis (Foxglove), for its seed-heads, both wild and cultivated (page 115 of the Florilegium)

Echinops (Globe Thistle), for its grey-blue, round, hedgehog-like heads (page 115 of the Florilegium)

Epimedium, for its attractive, long-stalked leaves (page 117)

Eryngium, especially *E. alpinum* and *E. tripartitum* (page 118)

Fœniculum vulgare (Fennel)

Gentiana, in all its forms, for its flowers

Geranium, in variety, for its leaves (page 120 in the Florilegium)

Helictotrichon sempervirens syn. *Avena candida*, for its tufts of blue-grey evergreen foliage

Hosta, in variety, for its leaves

Iris fœtidissima, the fresh flower arranger's "Goddess", which is equally important to the dried flower collector—this native "Gladwin" not only has evergreen leaves but comparatively magnificent flowers which leave us with an autumn splendour really worth waiting for. The opportune moment to watch for is the bursting of its heavily packed, buff seed-heads, filled with spectacular red berries. The seed-heads and their berries must be harvested immediately and plunged into the varnish, which should be waiting to receive them (this process is described in detail on pages 66-67). The genus is described on pages 124-125 of the Florilegium.

I. fœtidissima variegata, though not so free-flowering, has evergreen, cream-striped leaves, attractive for pressing

I. pallida variegata and *I. Pseudacorus* (the Yellow Flag Iris) produce beautiful cream and green striped leaves useful for pressing, and the latter also has good seed-heads

Isatis tinctoria, a crucifer of prehistoric origin—used for woad—which has impressive dark brown seed-heads

Lychnis chalcedonica (Maltese Cross, Jerusalem Cross), for its seed-heads

Monarda didyma "Cambridge Scarlet" (Oswego Tea, Bee Balm), for its long-lasting and most dependable seed-heads (page 128 of the Florilegium)

Pæonia, in variety, for its leaves and for some seed-heads (it is described in the Florilegium on pages 131–132)

Phlomis viscosa, for its unqiue seed-heads (page 134)

Rodgersia, for its panicled seed-heads and lovely leaves

Salvia officinalis (the culinary Sage) and kindred varieties, for delicate and most useful seed-heads (page 137); they appear in Fig. 9 on page 41

Scrophularia (Figwort), for its seed-heads, so useful as light gap-fillers in dried arrangements (page 138)

Thapsia villosa, an umbellifer with fantastically beautiful seed-heads, which comes from Northern Spain

BULBS

Many bulbous plants, especially the smaller species, provide the dried material collector with invaluable and most attractive seed-heads. Among them are *Muscari* (Grape Hyacinth) in variety—such as *M. tubergenianum*, *M. botryoides*, *M. azureum*, and *M. armeniacum; Tulipa* species; *Fritillaria* (Fritillary); *Scilla campanulata* (Spanish Bluebell); *Eranthis* (Winter Aconite); *Galtonia candicans* (Giant Summer Hyacinth); many lilies such as *Lilium auratum* and *L. regale*, the Bellingham hybrids, and some of the smaller species; and a number of *Alliums*—in particular the yellow *A. Moly*, whose flower dries splendidly if laid lightly in a flat open box and turned periodically to maintain its shape. *A. albopilosum* and *A. aflatunense* are also useful if the globular flower-heads are dissected for small arrangements. *A. nigrum* has a decorative seed-head. *A. pulchellum* is an attractive reddish-violet. *A. oreophilum Ostrowskianum* is a beautiful pink and dries well. Almost all these genera are described in more detail in the Florilegium. *Ornithogalum thyrsoides* (Chincherinchee) produces a white flower-head which dries well in preserving crystals and is most useful. Its great value to the dried flower arranger is exemplified by its appearance in many of the illustrations in this book—Fig. 19 on page 65 is one instance.

SILVER-LEAVED PLANTS

These superlatively beautiful plants give unique pleasure wherever they are seen, whether as a tall group in the back of a garden border, in front as an edging, massed on exhibition at a flower-show, in the market or the florist's shop, in a window-box, or growing wild in the fields. These lovers of the sun and open ground create a glistening eye-catching effect, and are real charmers in their varying shapes, and many of them thrive out of doors throughout the year. So long as sunlight and good drainage and, in individual cases, winter protection, are provided, their silver-white foliage and fascinating budding flowers (with the exception of the yellow daisy types!) are a joy quite unsurpassed. The flower assembler—whether of fresh or dried arrangements—will find them indispensable. Their cultural needs and sources of supply were most successfully set out by Mrs Desmond Underwood of Colchester whose book *Grey and Silver Plants* is well worth studying. As with other dried material harvesting, much depends upon the season for outdoor picking. Silver plants should be harvested early, just as they are reaching their prime and before any flopping, wilting, browning or curling occur. If they are grown in green-house or conservatory, the opportunities for picking are more extended; if growing in the wild, they should be ready in midsummer; they may be available in the florists, subject to market supplies; and they flourish the whole year through in window-boxes, or in urns and tubs on the patio.

Fig. 7: a big, complex arrangement in shades of white, off-white, cream and grey, with touches of pale green, set in a painted wood container of classic form. The centrepiece is a creamy-green dried hydrangea, and other hydrangea heads are recessed around it. Four clematis heads are set around the centrepiece: the fluffy bluey-grey pair appearing to the left above it and to the right below it, in a slanting line, were dried; the crisp spidery brown pair—above to the right and below to the left—were varnished (page 66). A third varnished clematis head is set low down, left of centre. Drooping in the mid-front are sprays of larch, covered with pale grey lichen. Small starry helichrysum flowers, with creamy petals and yellow daisy-like centres, are scattered through the arrangement. Spraying out from the centre is a mass of spear-shaped green eucalyptus leaves, bleached fern, hedgerow grasses, nipplewort and beautiful ballota with its small greeny-grey clusters clinging to a velvety stem.

For details of culture and hardiness, Mrs Underwood is an acknowledged authority. The drying and preserving of these silver-leaved plants is still open to experiment. Much will depend upon the particular season, and there will be a good measure of trial and error—but no-one, surely, could resist growing and picking for drying such gems as pearly little anaphalis, the artemisias, ballota (see Fig. 7 on page 37), the blue grasses of the *Festuca* species, the delicate santolinas, the decorative senecios, *Stachys lanata* (Lamb's Lug), and the rather tall and stately, soft to the touch, verbascum.

(There are several ways of preserving the silver-foliaged tribe:

1. by hanging the cut plant in its entirety—stems, leaves, flower-heads (in bud)—upside down;
2. by drying the same way, but spread out flat;
3. by pressing the cut plant, again in its entirety, between sheets of blotting-paper.)

SEEDS

A yearly order of annuals and biennials from a good seed specialist is essential. Messrs Thompson & Morgan of Ipswich (their address is given on page 155) have a most comprehensive seed catalogue with excellent preliminary notices and coloured illustrations of high quality. The following seeds, taken mainly from their list, may serve as a beginning; as the years go by, many others could, no doubt, be added.

Acroclinium syn. *Helipterum*, is a small, mainly pink everlasting of which there are several species. All are useful, but like all immortelles they *must* be picked just before the flowers open too widely. Gather them early on a dry day and hang them upside down to dry. Watch out for greenfly—high upon the stalks and at the base of the flowers—and remove it with the fingers before hanging the flowers to dry.

Agrostemma Githago "Milas" produces attractive slender seed-heads which look well when varnished (this should be done immediately after picking—the process is described on page 66). It is referred to on page 104 of the Florilegium.

Althæa rosea "Powder Puffs" (Hollyhock) is a new annual which is worth trying as it is smaller than the perennial species. Good for seed-heads and blooms for preserving. The genus is described on page 106.

Amaranthus: there are a number of variations listed, but *A. Caudatus viridis* (Love-in-Idleness), with its electric-green pendant racemes, is the most effective in muted arrangements.

Ammobium alatum grandiflorum (Sand Flower) is a charming white everlasting, with a yellow-turning-to-brown centre. It looks more attractive when picked and dried than when growing.

Antirrhinum (Snapdragon): before these bedding plants are put on the compost heap in the autumn, rescue any seed-heads worth drying. Hang them upside down.

Calendula officinalis (Marigold): a choice of flower-heads could be selected for preserving.

Clarkia produces some attractive seed-heads (this genus is described on page 112).

Delphinium (annual Larkspur) comes in various colours, but the white, the deep pink and the pale pink are among the most valuable flower sprays for drying. Gather while some of the buds are still unopened, thus making the most of their delicate tapering points. Pick on a dry day and hang immediately, heads downward. One can never have too many larkspurs in store. (The genus is described on page 114 of the Florilegium.)

Didiscus cærulea (Blue Lace-Flower) is a useful lavender-blue everlasting.

Digitalis (Foxglove): the annual garden variety "Foxy" is probably the most suitable as regards size. Among the wild foxgloves, *Digitalis purpurea* provides seed-heads of a more delicate and appropriate scale for dried arrangements.

Godetia is a popular annual, many of whose forms produce useful seed-heads for drying. It is described on page 121 of the Florilegium.

Gomphrena globosa (Spanish Clover), described on page 121, is a valuable everlasting with flowers in shades of purple, pink, yellow and white—a member of the amaranthus family.

Gypsophila is a popular annual which dries easily when stood upright. Only the single form should be grown as others are too heavy. It should be used very sparingly in dried arrangements, and then only for "insetting". As so little is required it is hardly worth garden space, especially as it can be found on the market in adequate quantity.

Helichrysum bracteatum (Straw-Flower) is an annual which is indispensable in dried flower arrangements. Mr George W. Smith, an internationally acknowledged authority on flower arranging, gives the following advice from his wide personal experience. "A genus of several everlasting species—but *H. bracteatum* is the half-hardy annual grown for drying. It has pretty double daisy flowers of a crisp straw-like appearance and originates from Australia. The straw-flower colour range has been much improved in recent years, and includes several soft tints of coral-pink, ivory, white and lemon, as well as the ubiquitous harsher maroons, gold and brown shades. To dry the flower-heads to perfection, gather each flower when the outer petals only are developed, and all the others are still closed over the boss of the stamen. It is futile to dry blooms which show yellow stamen centres as these will soon become overblown, discoloured and faded. Harvesting will commence with the first terminal bud and may continue throughout the growing season as ancillary side buds develop. These will be small blooms—a not undesirable feature in small decorations." Advice on wiring the blooms is given on page 87, and they feature in several of the assemblies in this book—Fig. 7 on page 37 is just one example; this arrangement includes a number of straw-flowers.

Ipomæa (Morning Glory) produces attractive groups of small seed-heads, which look well when varnished.

Matricaria eximia, syn. *Chrysanthemum Parthenium* (Feverfew) has white and yellow flower heads which dry well and are useful for "insetting" in arrangements. It is described on page 127 of the Florilegium.

Fig. 8: this collection of dried helichrysums, dried centaureas, and shaggy clematis seed-heads is backed by leaves and ferns. The slender spears of *Grevillea asplenifolia* thrust out on the upper right-hand side. *Adiantum* fern droops on the left, and there are other sprays on the right-hand side. Delicate feathery garden sage stands up at the centre back. The arrangement was assembled in a low dish.

Fig. 9: a rich, summer-style dried arrangement set in a stemmed sherry glass. Bright dried helichrysums and chemically-preserved zinnias are backed by pressed leaves, mixed pressed hedgerow ferns, delicate sprays of nipplewort and, at centre back, sage seed-heads from the herb garden.

Molucella lævis (the beautiful Bells of Ireland, also known as Shell Flower and as Molucca Balm) is not the easiest annual to grow, but well worth any amount of trouble to get it to succeed. The long stems of flowering, shell-like sheaths can be preserved in glycerine (pages 63-66) or can be hung upside down to dry. It is illustrated in Fig. 19 on page 65, and described on page 128.

Papaver: the double-flowered poppies, such as *P. Rhœas* and its varieties, *P. somniferum*, and so on, produce seed-heads in fascinating forms and colours. These are extremely useful and last for years. Some appear in Fig. 12 on page 48. The genus is described on page 132 of the Florilegium. Lay them flat in open boxes to dry.

Rhodanthe is a charming everlasting. *R. Manglesii*, syn. *Helipterum Manglesii*, *R. maculatum alba* and *R. m. rosa* are some of the most dainty and ethereal flowers for drying. With their beautiful buds, and delicately twisting stems, they add great lightness to any arrangement. Dry upside down, loosely tied so that they can retain their natural form.

Xeranthemum annuum is another everlasting of great charm. Its single and semi-double flowers of pink and mauve shades dry easily, upside down, and are invaluable for lending delicate character to an arrangement. It is described on page 143 of the Florilegium.

Zinnia: many flowers of this bedding plant can be successfully processed and mounted on false wire stems, as described on pages 84-86. They are invaluable for adding a variety of colour in the centre—and low down—in an arrangement, as illustrated in Fig. 9 which appears on page 41.

GRASSES

The infinite variety and decorative value of many different kinds of grasses, both cultivated and wild, gives the dried flower worker wonderful scope, adding interest, charm and lightness to an arrangement. There are corns, sedges, rushes and blade-like leaves, beautifully coloured and striped, and gracefully arching stems bearing plumed flower-heads. Some seed catalogues list mixed grasses for sowing. The Sunningdale Nurseries at Windlesham stock an admirable collection, many of which look well in the herbaceous border or wild garden. Sowings from packets of budgerigar and mixed bird seed can at times produce exciting "novelty" grasses, well worth the experiment. For a really exhaustive study of these specialised and charming forms of wild vegetation, consult *The Concise British Flora*, by W. Keble Martin.

Some of the most effective and decorative varieties, many of which can be treated as annuals, are listed below.

Agrostis (Bent Grass): this beautiful grass in its several varieties—all with fairy-like graceful inflorescences—is most people's idea of "real" grass; and indeed, nothing could be more indispensable to the dried arrangement worker. It is found abundantly everywhere in the wild and should be gathered early in the season and stored loosely, standing upright. No store should ever be without a supply. *A. nebulosa* (Cloud-Grass) is a fine garden form.

A. delicatula "Pouss" is a Bent grass of exquisite delicacy, from northern Spain.

Aira elegans (Hair-Grass), *A. caryophyllea* (Silver Hair-Grass) and *A. præcox* (Early Hair-Grass) have useful dainty decorative heads.

Alopecurus, in variety: some of these wild foxtails growing in damp ground have charming woolly inflorescence.

Apera spica-venti is known as Loose Silky Bent or Wind-Grass.

Calamagrostis canescens (Purple Small Reed), *C. epigejos* (Wood Small Reed) and other varieties, are all charming with their silky inflorescences.

Carex: a large genus of sedges, many of which are well worth collecting from their wild damp haunts. Some of their heads are beautifully coloured and are useful in dried arrangements for placing at the "central top", or drooping low, or as "insetting" lower down. Their leaves, too, are useful: some bright yellow, some striped, some nearly all-white.

Catabrosa aquatica (Water Whorl-Grass) grows in ponds, ditches and on moist banks, but is less abundant.

Cortaderia Selloana, syn. *C. argentea* is the very tall Argentine pampas grass with big grassy tufts and silvery plumes.

Festuca ovina glauca (Sheeps Fescue): its beautiful tufts of very narrow steel-blue leaves provide a most worthy addition to any dried group, especially small ones—a beautiful grass.

F. vivipara has very attractive green tufted ends.

Glyceria aquatica variegata has enchanting leaves, striped with yellow, and looks well when pressed and stored flat in blotting paper.

Helictotrichon sempervirens, syn. *Avena candida*, has narrow blue-grey leaves and graceful flower-heads which are both good for dried arrangements.

Luzula maxima, syn. *L. sylvatica:* much used in the garden as a ground-cover for suppressing weeds, *L. maxima* and other varieties of the *Luzula* genus of rushes are quite useful to the dried flower arranger for their brown flower-heads, and some are also useful for their leaves. It will frequently be found growing wild in woods, pastures, and on hills.

L. nivea is a pretty rush.

Melica ciliata L. comes from northern Spain and has creamy feathery seed-heads.

Milium effusum aureum (Wood Millet) has spectacular chrome-yellow leaves which can be pressed, as well as a particularly attractive flower-head which dries well stood upright with other fluffy grasses.

Miscanthus sinensis, syn. *Eulalia japonica:* there are various forms such as *M. s. variegatus*, *M. s. zebrinus* and *M. s. gracillimus*. The beautiful pinky-brown flower-heads can be dried either hanging upside down or lying flat, and the sheaves of green leaves—some tinged with yellow—press well. The leaves of *M. s. zebrinus* are banded cross-wise with yellow. For small arrangements, leaves can be cut into smaller lengths and their tips re-shaped into points before pressing and storing.

Molinia cærulea variegata (Purple Moor-Grass) is a pretty, variegated grass with cream-striped leaves (which need to be cut early as they die later) and purple flower-heads which are useful for drying.

Phalaris arundinacea picta (Ribbon-Grass, Gardener's Garters) has conspicuous white-striped leaves which press well. The flower-heads, too, are worth drying upright. The smaller form, *P. arundinacea* (Reed Canary-Grass), is useful. It was originally introduced as bird-seed.

Phleum pratense (Cat's Tail, Timothy Grass): a most useful and quite charming grass, growing wild in meadows. If harvested early, its heads retain their elongated shape, and with their beautiful light green colour make an attractive outline addition to dried arrangements. It appears, for example, in Fig. 26 on page 77.

Poa bulbosa var. *vivipara* is a tufted grass.

Stipa: though the ornamental *S. gigantea*, which grows some five feet high, is much grown in gardens and for decorative purposes, the smaller *S. pennata* (Feather-Grass), growing two and a half feet high, is more appropriate in scale for smaller arrangements. It appears in Fig. 19 on page 65.

For a further assortment of decorative grasses, many of which can be sown and harvested annually, consult Messrs Thompson & Morgan's seed catalogue. This and other catalogues will provide an exciting list. Examples are given below.

Avena sterilis (Animated Oats)

Briza—both *B. maxima* and *B. minor:* the Quaking Grasses which make such an intriguing, dangling addition to any arrangement

Bromus macrostachys and *B. madritensis*, with their attractive spikelets

Coix Lacryma-Jobi (Job's Tears)

Digitaria sanguinalis (Crab-Grass): an ornamental grass of recent production

Elymus arenarius (the beautiful Lyme-Grass) has stems from two to five feet high, glaucous leaves and impressive straw-coloured seed-spikes, so invaluable for arching effects, especially in tall arrangements. These spikes can be varnished (page 66), and their heads need to be dried flat.

E. canadensis: a graceful perennial with glaucous leaves and long seed-spikes, useful for tall arrangements

Eragrostis abyssinica, and *E. elegans* (Love-Grass)

Fig. 10: this assembly, set in a lacquered dolphin-stemmed container, was arranged one January day but glows like a June border. The special centrepiece of bright summer flowers—pink "Carol" roses, deeper "Garnette" roses and border carnations (all preserved in silica gel and then stored in Stemfix blocks, as shown on page 74)—is backed by tall spikes of pink larkspur, which were dried in the airing cupboard. The maple leaves span the Atlantic: some were gathered in Montreal, some picked up in Richmond Park in Surrey. The assembly is outlined with Spanish grasses.

Hordeum jubatum (Squirrel-Tail-Grass) and the wild barleys, with their characteristic beards which can be trimmed and shaped with fine scissors

Lagurus ovatus (Hare's-Tail-Grass—a most suitable name!), this creamy-hued piece of fuzzy fluff is quite the most popular, if not necessarily the most exclusive, of all grasses.

Pennisetum longistylum, syn. *P. villosum*, and *P. Ruppelii* syn. *P. orientale:* though somewhat tall, their long bristles are graceful. They are half-hardy and should be started off in a green-house.

Polypogon monspeliensis, a fine ornamental beard-grass of unusually attractive shape

Setaria glaucum, a half-hardy annual

S. viridis, the annual bristle-grass

Tricholæna rosea, a quite beautiful semi-fluffy grass. Its head, pink when first picked, ultimately takes on a lustrous grey colour—most fascinating for "outlining" in arrangements.

FERNS

The happy return to popularity of hardy ferns which can be grown in an otherwise difficult and almost uninhabitable shady garden corner where they can make such wonderful foils to hostas and other broad-leaved neighbours, means that collectors of material for drying should be in their element. Ferns of all kinds, shapes and sizes can form a most attractive feature in dried arrangements and should be grown as extensively as space will permit; they are valuable either fresh or preserved. Here again, however, a conflict of interests may arise between the gardener on the one hand, in defence of his precious collection of ferns which act as all-important, labour-saving "ground-cover" in his battle against weeds, and the floral arranger on the other hand, in quest of the beautiful green fronds which must be picked while the sap is still on the rise—and therefore well before they start to arch and spread in the heavy tangled mass which is perfect for ground protection!

Alternatively, of course, anyone picking ferns for flower arrangements, whether fresh or dried, will find much to delight him in the tender green-house and conservatory species which now, alas, are far less available than they were, being largely confined, when grown for decoration, to botanical gardens where the necessary tropical atmosphere can be provided.

The flower arranger, however, cannot afford to relax his pursuit of such a necessary commodity and will, if wise, exert all his efforts to obtain an ample supply. Fortunately there are now several authorities on the culture of cultivated ferns to whom he can refer: the Sunningdale Nurseries of Windlesham, Reginald Kaye Ltd of Carnforth, and Perry's Hardy Plant Farm at Enfield (full addresses are given in the list of addresses on page 154). All list the hardy ferns in their catalogues.

In wild life, the great fern families, such as *Filices*, are well worth exploring. It is a very large order, abundantly diffused over the surface of the globe, especially in moist climates (although some species are found growing in the chinks of rocks, in extremely hot climates). Great Britain, luckily, has a natural abundance of their riches, including such gems as *Adiantum*,

Asplenium (Spleenwort), the *Polypodium* genus (Polypody), *Polystichum Braunii* (Shield-Fern), *Cystopteris* (Bladder-Fern), *Ophioglossum* (Adder's-Tongue), *Botrychium* (Moonwort), *Phyllitis Scolopendrium* (Hart's-Tongue), and many more. The collector of these enchanting fronds requires a sharp penknife and a fine polythene bag in which to carry his harvest home, *flat*, before giving them a final pressing between sheets of blotting paper. With such a stock in store, the ultimate dried arrangement should be truly entrancing. This is especially true in the case of the tinier fronds—no more than a few inches high; they could be set in a carpet of club-mosses or selaginella or curly grey lichens, with a selection of wild grasses of the bent, timothy or rye types, and maybe some specially chosen seed-heads of winter aconites, grape-hyacinths, fritillaries or columbines—or why not a clump of blue gentians preserved in full bloom?

For illustrated descriptions of these wild ferns, there can be no better reference than Bentham's *Illustrated Handbook of British Flora*, Volume II.

MOSSES

Like ferns, happily now reappearing in many gardens, mosses (and lichens, which are described in the next sub-section) really require more attention than the cursory mention meted out to them here. They have been the cinderellas of the growing world for long enough, and the dried flower worker would do well to concentrate on making a collection of these fascinating plants, so invaluable for the base of arrangements.

For mosses such as quillworts, pillworts, club-mosses, selaginellas and others, reference should be made to Bentham's *Illustrated Handbook of British Flora*, Volume II.

LICHENS

Finally, there are the colourful lichens which clothe the roof-tops of old cottages and farm buildings and drape themselves in festoons along the branches of trees if the atmosphere is moist enough—as on the west coast of Scotland. Some of the types which need less moisture are found growing on rocks and boulders. All are very slow-growing, exceedingly varied in form, and extremely sensitive to atmospheric pollution—so they are not often found in in-dustrial surroundings. Harvesting lichens is probably best done with a knife, unless it is possible to sever intact portions of the branches upon which they are growing. These lichened branches—often of larch—can make the most enchanting arrangements (an example features in Fig. 7 on page 37). Lichens can be stored successfully, and when dry will last for years.

The study of lichen nomenclature would be a monumental task, and the collector could well be forgiven for avoiding it unless he wishes to specialise in lichen work. He should never, however, miss an opportunity of adding such varied and entrancing material to his store.

Fig. 11

Fig. 12

Fig. 13

Fig. 14

Four arrangements are grouped together on page 48.

Fig. 11, at the top left, is a traditional dried arrangement of mixed seed-heads and leaves, in shades of high summer green and autumnal browns and golds. Two shiny amber-gold clematis heads, dipped in varnish and then dried on newspaper, form a centrepiece. The ferns were picked from an old stone wall by the roadside and then pressed in blotting paper under a sofa cushion. Amongst the outlining material are sprays of nipplewort in the centre of the left-hand side, with its delicate green seed-heads on fine stalks, and timothy grass on the right-hand side.

Fig. 12 is an oblong arrangement, assembled in Plasticine on a flat cakestand, and set off by a frame of massed dark green leaves. In the foreground are creamy-yellow chincherinchees with their delicate, crowding, butterfly petals. In a spaced circle round these, pointing up the rich dark leaves, are dried yellow helichrysums. The beautiful blue poppy seed-heads, each with its own small golden-brown "crown", were dried flat in boxes. In the background are spires of reddish-green sorrel, and delicate pressed conifer sprays make a light outer frame beyond the dark crowding leaves.

Fig. 13, at the bottom left, is a light, feathery, dried arrangement, in a glass. The golden-yellow chincherinchee "sun" and the circling starry dried helichrysums are backed by roadside ferns, leaves and conifer sprays, and outlined with the delicate lacework of nipplewort and with garden sage. Low on the left is pencil-fine dried Bent grass.

Fig. 14, at the bottom right, is set in a white stemmed vase. The frontal feature is again a chincherinchee, surrounded and shown up by a spreading, star-shaped background of shiny, dark brown leaves of *Prunus lusitanica* (Portugal Laurel), glossy, formal and impressive. The deep dark colour of these pressed leaves is gently echoed by the spikes of reddish-brown sorrel which, with ferns, fine grasses, garden sage and the invaluable delicate seed-heads of nipplewort, spray out to form the rays of a lighter, more delicate background.

HARVESTING

Gather ye rosebuds while ye may,
Old Time is still a-flying:
And this same flower that smiles today,
Tomorrow will be dying.

Robert Herrick: *To Virgins, to Make Much of Time*

Introduction

For the arranger of dried plant material, to know what to grow, or at least to have an eye for where to find it, is all-important. It is, moreover, the very basis and wherewithal on which his art must depend. The same vital factor applies to harvesting: the arranger's perceptiveness, patience, knowledge, and, more important, his imagination and his desire to experiment, are of essential importance as he engages in a game of chance with Nature. The dried plant material collector, like the farmer and the gardener, relies on the harvest in any one year for the be-all and end-all of his trade. A precarious season can mean a depleted store and often a short supply of the one item most required. That is why the wise harvester should always seek to reinforce his stock in a good year, to insure, as far as possible, against a void after a barren one.

Harvesting continues to a greater or lesser degree throughout the year and may, in some cases, continue over a period of years. Vegetation is so singular and individual in its growing, so dependent upon its habitat and seasons, and sometimes, for no visible reason, so capricious in its temperament—and consequently in its harvesting—that this is always a matter for conjecture and compromise.

The Year's Programme

The New Year: the prospect for harvesting is not, perhaps, as bleak as the season might proclaim. Provided there is only a little snow, and not too much, or too severe a frost, there will be sprays of conifers and leaves of evergreens in plenty to pick. The gatherer will also have a splendid opportunity for seeking out some well-proportioned branches, and twigs which are delicate in outline. Several of the hardy ferns, especially those growing in old walls along the roadside, or in garden surroundings, will, if carefully selected, be quite suitable for picking and preserving. Mosses and lichens will also be ready to be collected at this time of year. The former need gentle handling or they may break into crumbling bits which are of little use. A small garden spade, a flat trowel, or a turf cutter would prove useful, or failing these, a kitchen fish-slice or large palette knife will make a handy moss-grubber. Collect the moss in all its many varieties, with as little soil as possible, and without letting it disintegrate or crumble. Lay it in a flat basket or seed-tray, and leave it to dry naturally. Trim it into shape for use as required. It is best used as a base for arrangements and can easily be glued or wired to the Plasticine setting material in the base of a container (such as an ash-tray or a saucer) to make a charming green ground for a small arrangement. Lichens can be handled in much the same way as moss, using only a kitchen knife or a large penknife. Lichen-covered branches of birch or larch look beautiful in dried arrangements and will last indefinitely. If there are some small cones on the branch, these will make it all the more entrancing.

With the coming of **spring**, and during the ensuing weeks, a watch must be kept for the delicate seed-capsules of the small species bulbs, especially *Tulipa* (Tulip), *Fritillaria* (Fritillary), *Muscari* (Grape Hyacinth), *Eranthis* (Winter Aconite), and—later—*Scilla campanulata* (the Spanish Bluebell). These all need to be picked as soon as the fragile seed-heads open, and then dried either standing loosely upright or lying in a flat open box. Some can be immersed in clear varnish, if desired (see page 66), and thereafter dried very carefully on a succession of clean sheets of newspaper. This takes only a few hours. Watch closely, so that the seed-heads do not become firmly stuck to the paper.

As spring gives way to **early summer**, so the harvester becomes more active, gathering seed-heads of *Aquilegia* (Columbine), *Iberis* (Candytuft), irises—Spanish, Dutch and other varieties, "Cottage" and "Darwin" and "Triumph" tulips, daffodils and the like. Some years produce better heads for preserving than others. All these heads should be harvested, if possible, when reasonably dry, but during a long wet season they should be harvested at any rate before they become sodden and black.

In **May**, the harvesting of grasses should begin, especially timothy and bent. Gather the grasses from the wild garden before the rotary scythe comes into action, and from the hedgerow before the mechanical cutters have ruthlessly trimmed the verges. The grasses in parkland and pasture and on the edge of cornfields will need watching, and so too will the wheat and barley heads—before the combines sweep the latter away. All grasses must be harvested before they begin to seed—in fact, as soon as the pollen count begins to rise. A grass in seed is useless for preserving unless it can be varnished in the very early stages, and this can only be done if its stem is strong enough to take the extra weight of the varnished head. Gather, whenever possible, on a dry day. Lay them flat (fluffy grasses excepted) and well spread out in boxes to dry. Wheat-heads look lovely and preserve best if varnished.

From late May onwards, and through the summer months, the collector should watch for seed-heads and cultivated grasses in herbaceous borders, in the wild garden, in the fields and along the hedgerows—and by the waterside. Some possibilities were mentioned briefly in the last chapter, and some are dealt with in detail in Part II. At the same time, attention must be given, almost daily, to the now ripening annuals, which have been sown either in groups along the garden borders or in rows in the "cutting only" portion of the kitchen garden. Here the collector must work continuously to effect quick harvesting of the opening flowers: helichrysums, for example, acrocliniums, rhodanthe, ammobiums, and other everlastings—and later, xeranthemums as they come into bloom, and the seed-heads of agrostemma—the latter especially for varnishing.

At this stage in the **high summer months** so much seems to be happening all at once—both in cultivated and wild life—and the harvesting of seed-heads is at its peak. No time must be lost. It is vital to harvest each bloom, each grass and each seed-head at the right moment. A delay of so much as a day, or even a few hours, in a difficult season can prove disastrous: the dishevelled, distorted remains will eventually disintegrate, and the leaves drop off. This is also the time to inspect the silken coils of the large-flowering clematis seed-heads and to gather some for immediate varnishing before they turn fluffy (varnished clematis seed-heads appear in several of the illustrations in this book; Fig. 7 on page 37 is one example). The right time for gathering actual flower blooms for processing is the latter part of the flowering period when the sap is still rising and, in the case of flower spikes, the top buds are as yet unopened. When gathering seed-heads, the capsules should be harvested as they are opening, and still crisp, and before the last seed is spent.

With the first signs of **autumn** the collector should have a slight feeling of relief. The bulk of the preserving should be well in hand and the store filling up. What remains is the harvesting of the autumn-falling deciduous leaves, the hydrangea heads (described in more detail in the next section), the berries, cones, and nuts, the ferns, mosses and lichens. The harvesting of evergreen leaves for pressing can go on throughout the year so long as the weather is reasonably dry and open.

Box, laurel, beech and other hedging shrubs should be picked before hedge-trimming begins—sprays of young beech leaves can be preserved at different stages in their growth by the glycerine treatment (see page 63). The later in the season this is done, the darker will be the resulting colour of the leaves.

Harvesting Hydrangeas

The harvesting of hydrangea heads frequently becomes an operation on its own, when most other plant material has long since been gathered in. Some of the beautiful flower-heads, or sterile bracts, will be ready for cutting before others on the same bush. The collector should keep an almost daily watch, brushing a hand gently and sensitively over the heads; in so doing

Fig. 15: wiring a hydrangea head: the stub wire is hooked over the delicate flower-head bracts. It is then bound into place with fine reel wire. Hydrangea flower-heads are nearly always split up into segments and mounted on wire stems. They can be used for infilling, as in Fig. 26 on page 77.

he will one day suddenly find that, in addition to changing colour, the sepal bract has become brittle, crisp to touch, feeling and sounding like crinkled tissue paper. Gather then, and only then, and finish drying in the store, standing upright with plenty of space between the heads. Some collectors hang them upside down with satisfactory results (Fig. 18 on page 61 shows some hydrangea heads drying in this way). Other collectors gather them earlier, during the late summer, place them in a vase of water, and allow them to dry out gradually, without renewing the water. (The dried hydrangea heads may be dissected into small pieces for lesser-scale arrangements, and false wire stems attached as shown above.)

Dried hydrangeas appear in a number of the arrangements illustrated in this book—for example, Fig. 26 on page 77. For the best varieties of hydrangea to grow, refer to page 123 of the Florilegium.

Other Material

Throughout the year, the harvester should keep a constant watch for suitable leaves and ferns, in the green-house, in the conservatory, among the house-plants, in florists' shops, nursery gardens, and markets—new material is always appearing on display, some of which would lend itself to pressing and preserving, either by glycerine or by chemicals. "Garnette" roses, zinnias, freezias, gentians and pompom dahlias come to mind—so too do the leaves of eucalyptus, grevillea, rhododendron, camellia—and so do the many ivies and ferns. There will also be dried material one can use—mostly the over-bleached or commercially processed grasses, stems and leaves, which should be scrutinised carefully, and very judiciously chosen. Plain skeletonised shadow leaves are charming, especially in company with flowers, grasses and seed-heads. Mosses and lichens can sometimes be obtained from florists.

Towards the Wild

The harvester who has a feeling in his heart for the incomparable loveliness of Nature should also turn his attention to the forest and the hills, the pastures and swamps, the marshes and the river bank. In such places, throughout the year, he will be rewarded a thousandfold by reaping the rich and plenteous harvest of the many wild plants which are equal, if not indeed superior, in beauty to their cultivated counterparts. These will most certainly provide him with an abundance for his store, including many gems as yet undreamed of. To list them individually would be an impossibility but once the collector has grasped the potential of the many preserving techniques, he should be encouraged to bring back his basketful with which to experiment, and by his successes should be inspired to cull still more from the realms of Nature's inexhaustible supply. A number of suggestions will be found in this book (more particularly in the Florilegium) but this is really only a means of "taking the horse to the water". One must leave it to him, if he thirsts, to drink, and drink deeply. A really exquisitely marked bramble leaf—a dangling alder berry—a fairylike arching sprig of larch, perhaps with lichen attached—a wild rhododendron spray with a promising bud—a frond of fine green bracken—a cow parsnip seed-capsule—a sorrel spike—a plantain head and a carpet of green moss: all these and many more are there for seeing, gathering, preserving and finally assembling.

All plant material, wherever it is to be found, has potential for the collector. Take plenty of risks—experiment, experiment, and again experiment. Never give up trying new seed-heads, different leaves, other flowers, more ferns and grasses. Dry them at different times and in different ways. If there are no records to learn from, all the more reason to set them—if there are no lines to follow, all the more reason to lay them.

Some Points to be Taken into Account when Harvesting

1. Avoid picking more than can be preserved at one go. **Flower blooms**, for example, must be carefully looked over for blemishes, insects, and other damage. (The majority of hollow-

54

Fig. 16: the author gathering a Golden Melody rosebud and a spray of its topmost leaves. The bud will be preserved by the chemical method described on pages 61 to 63, and the leaf will be pressed. She is using a pair of florist's stub scissors, and carries a wide wicker tray with sides to protect the contents from the wind.

stalked blooms will need to have a false wire stem inserted into the stalk to within half an inch of the flower-head. The bloom should then be laid in the preserving crystals—page 61—for the requisite number of days.) **Leaves** should be individually inspected back and front for insects, mildew or malformities before being placed between sheets of blotting paper and pressed beneath a sofa cushion. **Seed-heads** too require individual scrutiny, and so do **grasses, cones, berries, ferns and twigs** (the latter should be checked for canker). All this takes time, and should not be hurried just because the collector has gathered a mass of indiscriminate picking, bunched up in a hurry, which will inevitably end up on the compost heap.

2.   For successful harvesting pick **fresh flowers** while the sap is still on the rise but before the blossoms become full-blown. This is the case with delphiniums, larkspurs, roses, paeonies, zinnias, ranunculuses, pompom dahlias, and the like. **Seed-heads** should be gathered when fully ripe, just opening and crisp to the touch—poppy heads, for example, fritillaries, Spanish bluebells, tulip species, grape hyacinths and columbines.

To pick too early is as disastrous as to pick too late. In the former case the plant wilts in its immaturity; in the latter the blooms disintegrate, the leaves shrivel and the stems curl. Once again the compost heap is the only answer. (One man's meat is another's poison—so often the gardener, as opposed to the harvester, scores!)

3.   The actual picking is comparatively easy so long, as has been stressed, the collector does not attempt to gather too large a quantity all at once. A pair of sharp secateurs or florists' stub scissors, and a nice, wide, deep basket or a garden trug or skip, with sides to protect the contents from the wind (not the flat sort used by fresh flower arrangers), are all that is needed, with maybe a light cover of fine polythene to shelter the heads of clematis, centaurea and other fragiles.

4.   So far as harvesting is concerned, the dried flower arranger has a definite advantage over those handling fresh material. To begin with, there should not normally be any frantic hurry to pick before the sun shines too brightly or to catch the blooms before they open too much or become spoiled by rain or battered by wind. Though harvesting material for drying does depend more or less on a dry season, much can be done between those low pressure periods to collect flowers, grasses and seed-heads at one's ease, little and often, and the collecting of leaves, especially evergreens, can be carried on throughout the year. If it is necessary to pick in bad weather, a good sharp shake can do much to disperse dew, raindrops, frost or even snow; and hanging the harvestings upside down or lying them flat spread out on paper (ideally, blotting paper) will soon dispose of surface damp; and then the slow steady process of drying can continue unaided, provided the necessary conditions prevail (these are described on page 70).

5.   Before attempting to preserve any material by drying, pressing, chemical processing, and so on, it is essential that it should be in prime condition. Wrinkled, curled and wilting leaves and blemished flowers will be useless, except in rare circumstances when the "conditioning" process carried out by fresh flower arrangers can be resorted to.

Other Gathering Grounds

Finally, in the never-ending pursuance of material for preserving, there are other people's gardens (always provided, please, that permission has been sought). One happy example is the fantastically beautiful and very ancient Scottish garden, with its range of plants and leaves, at Marcus, Angus, my son-in-law's home, already referred to on page 10.

Those who travel abroad can also augment their store with exotics from other lands—opening up a vista full of exciting possibilities. The publication of *Wild Flowers of the World*, with text by Mr Brian Morley and wonderful illustrations by Mrs Barbara Everard, means that the collector has an excellent opportunity of widening the scope of his study. Why, after all, stick to a firmly "national" viewpoint? Many flowering plants are equally at home on both sides of the Channel, and indeed on both sides of the Atlantic. In the arrangement illustrated on page 65 (Fig. 19), crisp, glowing, dark brown seed-heads from Bermuda mingle happily with dried bladder campion from a Yorkshire hedgerow; and the chincherinchees in the same arrangement span a clear five thousand miles—some coming from England, some from far-off Kenya.

It is fun to pick and choose, to anthologise among growing things—some which are rare, some which are peculiar, others which are common, or others yet again which combine an exceptional loveliness of colour and form.

PRESERVING

Introduction

The process of drying and preserving should—indeed, must—start immediately after gathering. This is the basis of ultimate success in dried arrangements. Such an operation cannot be hurried—it must be allowed to take its own time. Neither must it be neglected—turning over, bending, coaxing, working or shaping the fragile items while they are drying can work wonders in helping to retain natural characteristics. The main essentials for drying are space, the right atmosphere and temperature (away from direct sunlight), and a sense of feeling in handling. Though constant and almost daily surveillance may be a counsel of perfection, any effort expended at this stage is well worth-while, and the results can last for months, and even years, giving pleasure far beyond the labour involved in attaining them.

A dry, airy corner in the basement, attic, stable or garage would do well; or, if possible, an outhouse or granary—dry, free from the attentions of mice, and with not too much direct sunlight—would be equally suitable. Failing these, the spare bedroom or boxroom will do, but never, please, the kitchen, wash-house or bathroom—steamy heat and lack of a free current of air cause wilting and mildew all too quickly.

There are several acknowledged methods of preserving plant material, and no doubt others are yet to be discovered. One important point for the collector to realise is that however meticulously instructions may be followed, and whatever special precautions may be taken, the process of preserving can, on occasions, turn out to be precarious—to say the least—and often fraught with frustration and disappointment. Nonetheless, with perseverance, trial and error, the venture will prove, more often than not, well worth-while, and the results can be unbelievably rewarding.

Experience with various methods of preserving plant material will reveal just how indefinite results can be, from one year to another. So much depends upon differing circumstances, and therefore so much is a matter of patient and painstaking experiment. No two seasons are ever quite the same—no two conditions can be relied upon to culminate similarly.

There are so many questions involved: changes of climate and of season over several years—snow, fog, rainfall and drought—prolonged cold or drying winds—soil structure—environment, exposure and shelter, and suitable growing positions: in fact, as fair a quantity of hazards as any gardener may be faced with. The dried material collector inevitably faces these same hazards and must concern himself with them. Though he does not necessarily have to grow the plants himself, he must perforce take the grower's difficulties into account when it comes to harvesting and preserving. By and large, however, the collector can call upon a series of alternative methods, and the following suggestions should be helpful.

Preserving Methods

HANGING UPSIDE DOWN TO DRY

Plants should be bunched together in small bundles. The bundles of heavier material should be tied with soft-textured string (never coarse string or elastic bands). Gardener's twine is better still—it is less likely to injure the stems while they are still fleshy. The bundles should then be suspended upside down (as shown below), from a beam or rafter or from a stout cord or garden line slung across from one end of the room to the other. Strong but soft-textured silk, fine twine, split raffia (glycerine-treated), or soft nylon thread should be used to tie the lighter and more delicate bunches, such as rhodanthe, helipterum, anaphalis, small seed-heads, and so on. A towel-horse, or even a coat-hanger, will probably be the most convenient and easiest means of suspending these. A bundle of Twist-its (from a horticultural sundries-man) is quite invaluable for keeping together some small, fragile treasures.

Material should not be bunched up tightly or in too large a quantity—this would result in the seed-heads or flowers becoming cramped or distorted during drying. Another point to remember is that as plant material dries, so the stalks shrink; consequently the "tie" (wire, twine, and so on) will require periodical gentle tightening—otherwise there will be a pathetic little heap of blooms come adrift and shrivelling on the floor below.

HOT AIR DRYING

Blooms which need quick drying in order to retain their colours do best in a hot-air cupboard, either suspended upside down on wire, or spread out carefully on paper on a shelf. Delphiniums and larkspurs definitely need this treatment, and it is possible that others might respond satisfactorily as well. This process should only take a few days at the most, depending on the heat and the condition of the blooms. Check frequently. The material should be removed from the cupboard as soon as the petals sound like crinkled paper when touched. Thereafter, the blooms should be stored upright, in containers without water, in a dry atmosphere and away from sunlight, until required.

DRYING FLAT

For smaller and more fragile material (flowers, seed-heads, and so on), drying flat on trays, in open boxes, or on large flat sheets of brown paper laid on the floor or the table, proves very successful. This method should also be used for drying long grasses such as squirrel-tail-grass, rye-grass, broom-grass and timothy grass, for wheat, barley, and so on, and for many others whose heads would otherwise become too heavy for their slender stalks.

DRYING UPRIGHT

Some plants with rounded inflorescence, like *Alchemilla mollis*, some of the umbellifers, such as fennel or cow parsley, and others which are similar in form, will dry more easily standing upright, loosely, with plenty of space between each head, in vases or other containers, with no water. Deep cartons or plastic buckets are particularly useful. This method of drying must be used for all the genera of fluffy-headed grasses, such as *Festuca*, *Glyceria*, *Agrostis*, *Briza*, *Tricholæna* and the like. Bundles can, if necessary, be tied with fine plastic-covered wire, so long as it does not harm the stems. This wire can be bought in large circular rolls.

DRYING BY PRESSING

Sprays of leaves, such as grevillea, box, osmanthus (now known as *Siphonosmanthus Delavayi*), and fresh, single leaves of all shapes—laurel, for example, rhododendron, paeony, elaeagnus, iris, and montbretia—and ferns in all their species, should be dried by very gentle and prolonged pressing. Harsh treatment such as clamping between heavy weights, or under heavy books (or between their pages, which may be damp and airless), should never be used. Rather should they be placed between sheets of blotting paper and pressed lightly in suitably porous conditions—beneath a flat sofa cushion, for example, or an unused bedroom mattress—where they can continue to breathe and so retain much, if not all, of their original texture, colour and form. It occasionally happens that the blotting paper becomes soggy—much will here

Fig. 18: a view of the granary, where the "industry" began. In the immediate foreground is a huge bowl of fir cones. Ranged behind this are tall vases, some containing umbellifer seed-heads and grasses which are drying upright. A beautiful arc of acanthus hangs from the beam. Beyond this, to the right, are bunches of sorrel seed-heads hung to dry, and beyond this again, at the very right of the illustration, are strings of hanging hydrangea heads.

depend, as so often in the course of the preserving processes, on the conditions in each particular case; should dampness occur, fresh blotting paper should be carefully substituted.

Pressing with a hot iron is ultimately unsuccessful and should be deplored—Nature in all its infinite beauty and grace was never intended to be so abused.

Provided that sufficient time can be allowed—a minimum of six weeks—drying by gentle pressure will prove more than adequate for all foliage and ferns, and they can then be stored for many years.

CHEMICAL DRYING PROCESSES

The chemical processes of drying—or, more precisely, preserving—can be used for individual blooms. An airtight container, such as a biscuit tin or a plastic box, will be needed (a good quality cardboard box could also be used). Some flower-heads—helichrysums, dahlias, zinnias, roses and gentians—are best wired before preserving (a special section on wiring appears on pages 84-86).

The blooms should be carefully immersed in whatever drying chemical is used, and the container should then be sealed with sellotape and left undisturbed for a number of days— the exact period will depend on prevailing conditions, as dampness, heat and so on will all affect the length of time the blooms take to dry. It takes anything between twenty-four hours for lilies-of-the-valley, to three or four days for hyacinths, roses, lilac, wallflowers, broom and many others.

Finely ground crystals of silica gel are good drying agents. They must be re-heated in a moderate oven after use, in order to re-activate their preservative properties. Other drying agents, in capsule or granulated form, can be procured from chemists, but they are really only useful to spread around the store in order to maintain a dry atmosphere.

The drying agent Stemfix supplied by Stemfix Accessories Ltd (whose address is in the list on page 154) is singularly successful and easy to use, and is thus well worth a trial. It can be re-activated a number of times and so it has economical advantages.

In the first edition of this book, advice given by Garden Specialities of Leigh-on-Sea, describing the use of their drying agent, was quoted, with their kind permission; although this particular mixture is not currently available, their comments are of abiding interest. "A certain amount of shrinkage occurs," they wrote, "but this does not detract from the fresh living look of the flowers. Timing is important for success, and because the texture and maturity of the flowers affects the moisture content of the petals, a bit of experiment is necessary. Usually it is wise to test the flowers after two or three days in the mixture, to see if they feel crisp to the touch. If not, additional time will be needed. If left in the powder too long, flowers will dry so much that petals will drop. Some flowers, like zinnias, take only two days to dry adequately, while snapdragon, which is dried on the stalk, takes six. Flowers of the same kind vary in drying time, depending on maturity."

Any firm usually gives detailed instructions for use, including some directions on how to immerse the flowers in the mixture (the blooms should not touch one another), and advice on how to check whether the drying process has been satisfactorily completed. "Test for dryness by pouring off the mixture slowly, to uncover one flower only. If this appears to be adequately dry and crisp to the touch, pour off some more of the compound, and gently lift out the flowers. If some seem to need additional drying, lift them to the top of the mixture, to remain in the closed container two or three days longer—then remove, shake gently, and dust off any adhering granules."

The blooms should then be set to "air" in Stemfix foam—Fig. 24 on page 74—while awaiting assembly: a method of storing which ensures that the flower-heads will not be damaged or crumpled.

It is advisable not to mix the varieties of blooms in a container, since different kinds of flowers will take different lengths of time to dry.

It is possible, say firms selling drying agents, to preserve about ninety per cent of all flowers on their natural stems, so long as a suitable container is available—but for the type of small arrangement predominantly discussed in this book, it is unnecessary to preserve more than the first inch or so of the stem, as false wire stems are easier to bend into arching or curving shapes in the container. (The wiring process is described on pages 84–86.)

GLYCERINE TREATMENT

Glycerine treatment is excellent for branches and sprays of trees and shrubs. (They should first be trimmed to an attractive shape, and any superfluous "out-of-line" or imperfect leaves removed.) It is also useful for large leaves like bergenia or elongated leaves such as aspidistra, and for green-house foliage and foliage from overseas. Beech, sycamore, rhododendron, elaeagnus, hornbeam and maple, together with their seed-heads, come to mind—also montbretia, iris, and eucalyptus, and an infinite number of others. On the other hand, some leaves, like lime, are too thin or fragile, and others again, like *Viburnum rhytidophyllum*, too tough. Experiment and trial from one season to another may prove well worth-while and should help the collector to enlarge his experience. All very fine, delicate or feeble leaves should be dried by pressing.

The following instructions have been kindly provided by Mr Brian J. Withill, from Yorkshire. The memory of his impressively graceful sprays of glycerined foliage in many of the arrangements displayed in the York Minster Flower Festival in 1967, will remain life-long with all who saw them.

"Many deciduous and evergreen shrubs or plants or branches will respond to preservation by the glycerine treatment. They will change colour, but have advantages in that they retain a supple, pliable nature and an attractive textural appearance.

"Pick mature green foliage, choosing attractively shaped sprays free from insect blemishes. Trim away any lower leaves likely to be submerged, and crush or split the stem ends for about two inches. Prepare a solution with one-part glycerine to two-parts near-boiling water; this warm solution is more readily taken up by the foliage. Stand the sprays of leaves in about six inches of solution, using a vessel which will not tip over easily. Leave in a cool dark place for two to three weeks. Frequent inspection will indicate how well the leaves are taking up the solution and whether or not topping up is necessary. The leaves will turn from green to dark brown, and their undersides may appear slightly oily, indicating that they are fully preserved and require no further moisture. They can be stored in a cool dry place in empty vases, until needed.

"It is important to note that these directions are for the preservation of beech and other deciduous tree foliage, such as oak, whitebeam, and sweet chestnut. The length of time required in the glycerine solution will vary enormously and only experience will tell. As a rough guide, the tougher the leaf, the longer it needs. On this basis, seed-heads of wild *Clematis vitalba* (Traveller's Joy), molucella and eucalyptus leaves may only require one week, whereas evergreens such as camellia, laurel, aspidistra and fatsia may need considerably longer—up to six or ten weeks. A stronger solution—about half and half—is recommended for these tough leaves. If large quantities are to be treated, it is wise to try to purchase bulk crude glycerine rather than the more costly refined type available from chemists.

"For the more adventurous, the total immersion method produces good results with leaves which do not normally respond by drinking up the mixture. Shallow tanks of solution are needed. Fronds of green bracken, leaves of *Grevillea robusta* and individual ivy leaves can be preserved. Care should be taken to inspect them each day, as once they have turned brown they should be gently washed free of surplus solution and laid to dry out in a warm place, on blotting paper. Many imported leaves are preserved in this way—hence their high cost of production; but as they are almost indestructible, given reasonable care, they are well worth the price. Magnolia, loquat, *Hibiscus tiliaceus* (the Mahoe Tree) and dracaena are all useful.

"The variations of brown are innumerable, and one batch of leaves will vary from another, much depending on the strength of the solution, and on the individual plant. It is

Fig. 19: fresh and dried material are combined in this graceful, swirling arrangement, an example of the "three-dimensional" style, which was created on a frosty February day in a London flat. The fresh black-eyed chincherinchees (the two big creamy-petalled flower-heads, one centre left and the other slightly to the right of the centre back) were a gift from a friend newly returned from Mombasa. They are set off by long sprays of variegated ivy from the balcony; by fresh veronica at right lower centre, also picked on the balcony; by *Grevillea asplenifolia*—again fresh (the long sword-like green leaf springing to the right of the centre back); by sprigs of fresh green on either side; and by an assortment of dried material in shades of cream, brown, and green, selected from the store. The frilled green spike at centre back is dried *Molucella lævis* (the beautiful Bells of Ireland). To the left and lower right of this are sprays of dried astrantia (creamy-grey clusters spaced on slender stems); and immediately in front of the *Molucella lævis* and spraying on the left, ballota can be seen. A drift of dried border pinks, with creamy-caramel petals, arches across the arrangement. Dried chincherinchee clusters beside the fresh, low in the centre. To the left of the fresh chincherinchee are the crisp brown bell-heads of dried *Silene Cucubalus* (Bladder Campion) from the hedgerows of Yorkshire; and behind and below this are dried seed-heads of *Centaurea dealbata*, like silvery-fawn flowers. Curving below and above the fresh chincherinchee are dried dark-brown seed-heads from Bermuda. The small fluffy cream sprays curling out to mid-right and lower right of the central cluster are dried *Clematis Jouiniana*. The dried seed-heads, with long stamens thrusting out from upturned spiky bells, came from Mombasa. Light feathery strands of *Stipa* grass fill in at the back. The arrangement is set in Oasis and wired into a bowl pinholder.

possible, however, to fade some glycerined leaves artificially, by placing them in strong sunlight—this sometimes produces a pale tan colour in certain leaves, such as beech, or a pale honey in aspidistra.

"One word of warning: foliage which has been too long in the solution will exude drops of glycerine and moisture on the surface of the leaf and may even turn mildewed in odd damp places. This is why it is advisable to store or display the finished product in a warm airy position. It can be washed and dried when surface dust spoils its appearance.

"A question often asked is whether it is possible to preserve autumn-tinted leaves, such as maple or beech, by this method. The answer is no, as in this process the leaves have to drink up the preservative—and once a growing leaf begins to turn colour, one knows that the flow of sap to the leaf is terminating; that, after all, is the reason for the colour change. Tinted leaves can only be preserved by pressing" (which was described on pages 60-61).

VARNISHING WITH CLEAR VARNISH

This method can be very effective. It is most suitable for berries and seed-heads. Large clematis seed-heads—"Nellie Moser", "Barbara Dibley", "Mrs Cholmondeley" and others— the wild rose bay willow-herb, empty seed-vessels of bladder campion, and seed-heads of montbretia and corn cockle look especially charming when preserved in this way, It is, how- ever, essential to varnish clematis and willow-herb seed-heads *immediately* after picking, before they turn fluffy. The method is also useful for preventing seeds from opening, and preserves intact plantains, grasses (other than fluffy types), corn, the exquisite dangling seed-heads of the birch tree, sycamore keys, and plane tree berries. Varnishing unopened buds such as xeranthe- mum, clematis, helichrysum, centaurea, and the wild knapweed can be most effective, and they make entrancing additions to smaller arrange- ments. Once the collector has tried the clear varnishing method, it will undoubtedly lead him on to further experiments.

Any general-purpose *clear* varnish (Valspar, Permoglaze and others like them) will do, so long as it is completely transparent. When var- nishing tall sprays such as rose bay willow-herb, lily seed-heads and long grasses, purchase the varnish in quantity and pour it into a tall, narrow container, shaped like an agricultural drainpipe standing on end—such a container is shown in

Fig. 20: the drainpipe container which holds the varnish. It is approximately twenty inches deep and eight inches in diameter.

Figure 20. (With any luck the local ironmonger would solder one of tin, zinc or other rustless metal, open at one end, and with a handle.) The plant material is dipped, head downwards, in the varnish and then held to drain for a few minutes until ready to be placed gently on sheets of paper to dry. After use, the varnish should be strained, if necessary, and returned to its tin, which should be well sealed. There is no need to clean or rinse the "drainpipe". (Varnishes are generally highly inflammable, so due precautions should be taken; and it might be advisable to experiment with a small quantity first—especially if working in a small closed area—since some collectors may find they are allergic to certain varnishes.)

Skeleton or Shadow Leaves

Though there are several ways in which leaves—tough glossy leaves with woody fibres, such as magnolia, camellia, ivy, holly, and so on—can be skeletonised, these shadow leaves are not needed in large quantities in the small dried arrangements being described, so the somewhat messy and unpleasant process entailed is not advocated here. Attractive, transparent leaves can be obtained in different sizes from specialist florists. If no small leaves are available, large leaves can be cut into two or three parts and re-shaped for wiring according to requirements. If the leaves are too stiff, they can be moulded gently between the fingers, or curved around a pencil to give a more natural effect.

Summary

To sum up, two basic points in the preparation of dried material can be stressed.

1. The process of drying, pressing or preserving by chemicals *must* start immediately after gathering; delay of more than a few hours can, in some cases, result in disaster.

2. There can be no hard and fast rule for the general technique of drying and preserving —it is all a matter for thinking out, and trial and error experiment. No two plants are alike in structure, vigour, vitality—no two drying conditions are completely similar—no two districts, climates or atmospheres can be said to be beyond variation. Much must be left to on-the-spot discretion—to a feeling, as it were, for the possibilities of the material, an understanding of its capriciousness, its whims and fancies, and a desire to conserve its own form, character, colour and charm.

At this stage in the process of growing and harvesting, successful preserving becomes a challenge demanding intuition and foresight, imagination and vision. No two seasons, no two moments, are ever quite the same; consequently each individual result will be unique.

STORING

Great store of flowers, the honour of the field.

Edmund Spenser: *Prothalamion*

Introduction

And now to storing—a most important phase in the dried arranger's calendar, when the preparation of the material is almost complete and when the final and culminating stage comes into sight—and a reminder too that "Nature is ever returned double to us, she is the preserver and treasurer of beauty." What more can one ask for, except the gift to display her treasures? What more can Nature supply, except still further enticement to explore her realm?

This then is the moment when the results of months of growing and harvesting and preserving stand ready for the final display—a moment too for the worker to survey, to reflect, to wonder, and indeed to be thankful—in truth, the season of Harvest Thanksgiving. They are all there: the leaves, the ferns, the grasses, the flower-heads, the seed-pods, the branches, the berries, the cones, the mosses and lichens—all this natural beauty is preserved for the arranger to pick and choose from, and he pauses—*reculer pour mieux sauter*—awaiting the moment of inspiration to achieve assembly.

Assembly: maybe for some particular occasion—an especially pleasing container just asking to be filled—a spur-of-the-moment gift—"just something" to enliven a dark corner when fresh flowers are scarce—or perchance for the sheer delight of arranging a little assembly of one's own favourite things: all here, collected together in one's own Aladdin's Cave.

Fig. 21: a comparatively small arrangement made for a friend to match her room. It was not easy to find so much blue (often a difficult colour to collect). The blue gentians, cornflowers and larkspur were a happy "find", with small pink roses, rhodanthe, purple statice and silver leaves, and mauve xeranthemum. The green background was a small form of eucalyptus, and the fern was also rather special.

The main object of the store is to keep the season's harvest (including, too, any treasured left-overs of bygone seasons) in as near perfect a condition as possible. The arranger must safeguard against any hint of distortion, or loss of colour or shape, or developing brittleness, and against any inclination to shrivel and curl. This store is beyond price to the arranger for it not only represents the results of seasons of planning, growing, harvesting and preserving, but is also the treasury of the very materials which ultimately determine the difference between failure and success.

Principal Features of the Store

Ideally the store should be a place set aside for this specific purpose: an outhouse, a granary, a disused garage, a storeroom, an attic, or a good part of the worker's studio.

CLEANLINESS

This is essential for the safe-keeping of the treasured collection. A large dustbin should always be at hand for unwanted trimmings, decayed leaves, mis-shapen seed-vessels, faded flowers, and so on, and for sweepings from table or floor. This should be emptied regularly. A generous use of light polythene sheeting and bags is the best means of controlling dust, and large sheets of paper or flat boxes will help the dried flower worker to prevent the spread of endless seeds during storage.

GUARDING AGAINST HUMIDITY

Damp is the storer's greatest enemy. In less than no time it can cause mildew, canker, wilting and discolouration—and final disintegration. It must be avoided at all costs, and some form of heating, however meagre and occasional, should be on hand when necessary.

AIR

An airy atmosphere is important. An enclosed attic or closed garage needs regular opening up to encourage the circulation of air.

HEAT

Heat is only necessary in so much as it may be required to maintain dryness. This purpose apart, it can be harmful.

LIGHT

Neither too much light nor too little should be the aim. Complete darkness is not good, and direct sunshine pouring in, unshaded, would be fatal.

GUARDING AGAINST RATS, MICE, FLIES, INSECTS

These must all be guarded against. Greenfly can multiply rapidly if not checked by hand-picking or spraying.

THE DANGER OF MILDEW

Mildew must be carefully watched for, especially on pressed leaves and on some seed-heads. If an item becomes infected, one can try to check the mildew by applying a coat of varnish, but more often than not, it must be thrown out.

Storage

For the actual storage of individual items, a supply of long, wide, **florists' boxes**, with lids, is by far the best. These are strong and light, and nearly always have air-holes already. They can be labelled and stacked for easy access. Wide, flat **dress-boxes** can be used, if sufficiently strong and of good enough quality, but they are inclined to absorb moisture and become damp, and should not be used with the lids on. For upright storage, **wine merchants' cartons** (the deep kind) are essential. They are light and easy to stack when not in use.

When preserving leaves, a plentiful supply of sheets of **blotting paper** (in varying colours to denote the grouping of the contents) should be available. These sheets, with their dried contents, can be stacked carefully on top of one another—open ends towards the worker—in a safe corner, ready for use. They can be labelled, if required, by using Sellotape-X in differing colours, and descriptive lettering—this saves much lengthy searching for the right leaves during assembly, and avoids constant harmful disturbance of the fragile collection.

Rolls of clear **cellophane or polythene** should be stocked in the store:

1. for spreading lightly over material lying flat in boxes;
2. for covering lightly material in the upright drying position—*fluffy grasses definitely excluded*; and
3. for use in packing arrangements.

Fig. 22 and Fig. 23: the two dried assemblies shown overleaf were created for St Peter's, Eaton Square, London. That on the left, named "Heaven and Earth"—and captioned by the Rev. Fr D. B. Tillyer, Vicar of St Peter's (whence was borrowed the very appropriate brass pitcher)—is intended to depict the relationship between Heaven and Earth. The red maple leaves represent those living now, the skeletonised magnolia leaves those who have gone before us. Their inter-action within the one arrangement symbolises the communion between us in the Church. The assembly on the right (the first done for St Peter's) is known as "Worship". It stands beneath one of the arches to the right of the high altar. Its main feature—all muted white— is based on the beautiful long sprays of *Helychrisum peliolatum*, white larkspurs, roses and rhodanthe, and some silver leaves.

The Rev. Fr D. B. Tillyer writes: "Christians believe the Word which was made flesh in Jesus Christ is the same Word through whom God created the world. Creation and redemption are two aspects of God's undivided grace. Jesus institutes the sacraments by which God's natural gifts convey supernatural graces to man. Thus, the sacraments pre-figure the day when God will transfigure all things with His glory: and so may all created things, if they are dedicated to the service of God. An arrangement of dried flowers, with a suitable title and perhaps a few words of caption, becomes not only a source of beauty but also a bearer of God's grace, conveying a vision of divine glory. Certainly, this is what the author's dried flower arrangements have brought to my own church."

Fig. 24: a close-up view of the work-table and the shelf immediately behind it. On the table a collection of varnished bladder campion and centaureas is "airing" in blocks of Stemfix foam. A shortened version of the "drainpipe" container for varnishing stands at the back. This container should really be a good three feet deep so that long grasses, rose bay willow-herb seed-heads and lily heads can be dipped into the varnish before being laid to dry on sheets of newspaper. Other equipment on the table includes a bundle of stub wire, a pair of stub scissors, and a special pedestal (the latter is a favourite of the author's and was used for all the arrangements shown in this book; but anything similar would do—an upside down container would be perfectly adequate). It is best when assembling to have the arrangement slightly (about two inches or less) above eye level. Flower-heads which have been preserved in silica gel are "airing" in Stemfix blocks on the shelf. This means of storing them ensures that they do not become damaged or crushed. Amongst them are delicate blue trumpets of gentian, "Garnette" roses, and narcissus flower-heads with their golden corollas. Other bunches of fragile flower- and seed-heads have been hung to dry from the topmost shelf.

Cellophane or polythene bags should also be available, in which to keep and transport delicate items, and for a wide variety of purposes, such as storing damp mosses.

Large sheets of **brown paper** are useful when drying items laid flat on the floor or on trestle tables—they can help to control the spread of seeds during ripening and drying.

Large sheets of **newspaper**—in ample quantities—are necessary when varnishing. These should be replenished frequently, and the sticky portions thrown away.

Soft-textured string or gardener's twine will be needed for tying heavier bundles which are hung to dry upside down; **strong soft silk, soft nylon thread, fine twine or split raffia** for the more delicate bunches; **Twist-its** for the most fragile harvestings; and **fine plastic-covered wire** for tying bundles which are to stand upright. (A special section describing suitable tying materials appears on page 59, in the chapter on preserving.)

Stemfix foam will be useful in the store, since delicate blooms which have been preserved by the chemical process can be set to "air" in it (Fig. 24 above shows this well). Stored in this way, they retain their individual shape and the fragile petals are not distorted.

Fig. 25. in the foreground an assortment of leaves and grasses is drying flat. Behind them are various trays, boxes and buckets of other dried material. On the table at the back grasses and seed-heads are drying upright. Two completed arrangements stand on the topmost shelf, with an assortment of small individual containers arranged beneath them. Notice particularly the varnished clematis seed-heads which are lying in a box in the foreground.

(The equipment that the collector will need when **harvesting** is described on page 56; the "mechanics" for **assembly** are listed on pages 78–83, the wiring and binding materials on pages 84–86, and equipment for use when **packing** arrangements, on pages 97–98.)

Conservation

Never ever hand over the discarding of a fresh arrangement (admittedly past its best) to anyone who may not have an "eye" for retaining the unshrivelled bits and pieces. Put them in their separate places in the store for further use as and when needed.

"The Painter's Palette"

Assuming these recommendations are followed successfully, there should be no reason why most of the precious stock should not be kept in good order for several seasons—leaves, grasses and ferns will last for many years. It is important to keep in store a few bits and pieces to act as spare parts for replacing and replenishing at any time. This is an integral part of the venture, and given the necessary space and conditions, should not be too difficult to achieve.

Such a store of colourful materials, all ready and prepared for use, is like a painter's palette, and a constant joy and inspiration to the artist—whether he is working with paints or with dried plant material.

ASSEMBLY

It is not enough to love flowers to arrange them well . . . it is necessary to work . . .
to be rarely, very rarely satisfied, to think, and imagine, and try again and again.

Constance Spry: How To Do The Flowers

Introduction

Theoretically, assembly is a bringing together of all the resources and miscellany of material so painstakingly mustered throughout many precarious seasons, many long months, and maybe, several years. If the preparation has gone well this stage, with the galaxy now ready for assembly, can be the most exciting feature of the whole process—a moment indeed, when artistry can combine with the skill of arranging in achieving the final endeavour.

For the floral arranger, be he working with fresh or dried material, this is the most challenging stage in the whole process of his art. Earth's gleanings lie, literally, at his feet, and in his hands rests the power to evoke pleasure in those for whom he creates, and to enhance with his talents an art as yet not fully appreciated in this rather ersatz age.

In assembly, there are so many delights to exploit: a particularly beautiful specimen of leaf—a fragile skeleton seed-capsule—an attractively curved branch—some appealing twiggly bits—or a specimen "centrepiece" flower. Material can be grouped to be in accord with some individual need—to be in harmony with an especial project—or to be "just so right" for one exceptionally demanding occasion.

In all undertakings, theory and practice should ultimately find their meeting-place and join together; in the matter of dried arrangements this is particularly true. Ideally the dried flower arranger should be both a gardener and an ecologist, with practical background knowledge, and a consequent feeling for how the material grows—whether tree, shrub or plant, wild or cultivated—so that it may be set in as natural a way as possible in the ultimate assembly. On the other hand, however, intuition can transcend a multitude of obstacles and artistry complete a perfect picture, so long as it is free from too many inhibitive rules and unfettered by excessive conventionalism.

Fig. 26: this muted but rich arrangement is designed around the beautiful centrepiece of blue-green dried hydrangea heads. The crisp brown whirls of the varnished clematis heads and the dried centaurea flower-heads contrast with the delicate massed hydrangea petals. On the extreme right at the back are the sword-shaped leaves of celmisia, inserted back to front to give a silvery effect. A pale green head of timothy grass protrudes delicately on the upper left.

In the type of small-scale dried arrangement mainly discussed in this book—something in the range of 26 inches high and 24 inches wide, or less—the arranger should contrive to make his arrangement as secure, and therefore as durable, as possible, for one of the great assets of the arranger's art, and one of the objects of his craft, is to create an arrangement which will last for several years and which can be moved without harm from place to place.

Mechanics

Successful and enduring assembly (and this includes both fresh and dried material) depends first and foremost upon the "mechanics"—the framework upon which an assembly is based. This should be in tune with the chosen container and equally appropriate to the material to be used. Aesthetically, the mechanics should be wholly self-effacing, while at the same time, and at all costs, utterly secure—and this principle applies to every type and to every scale of arrangement.

The main relevance of these comments, however, requires definition. Although the principles mentioned above are the same, with appropriate variations, for any size of assembly, the remarks which follow are mainly intended to apply to the smaller, but by no means necessarily miniature, type of arrangement—something of the kind which is, so to speak, "mobile", and which can be moved easily from one position to another, or maybe transported, with due care, to a friend or anyone else interested, for a special purpose.

Basically, the mechanics consist of any utilitarian accessories which may be used to fix the dried (or fresh) material in the desired position in the container, vase, or other form of receptacle. In dried flower work, these mechanics include the setting material (such as clay or Oasis), stub or reel wiring, Sellotape, and any other devices employed for securing the entire arrangement invisibly. Fig. 28 on page 83 shows a collection.

SETTING MATERIAL

Although clay and wax and their various compounds are occasionally used, it would seem that Plasticine, Plastone or other similar materials now on the market, are the most successful. They are clean and easy to handle and give the arranger the opportunity of repositioning any items during, or even at the end of, assembly as most of them harden gradually; and, in the case of small arrangements, they provide adequate weight and utter security.

The use of crumpled chicken-wire, pin-holders, cones or such devices, so inseparable from fresh flower arranging, is not advisable for this type of dried assembly; and Oasis, Floropak and kindred products are likewise neither sufficiently firm nor long-lasting in their dry state—nor indeed have they enough weight. Sand can be put at the base of the container, up to about one-third the height of the bowl, and Plasticine firmly wedged on top. This adds weight and is economical in Plasticine. Should the sand be damp, delay adding the Plasticine until the sand has dried; otherwise a vacuum may ensue between the two. Some arrangers use pebbles instead of, or as well as, sand, but this could prove less stable.

When the Oasis or Plasticine is in position, it should always be covered with moss, lichen or reindeer moss, fixed with thick hairpins or bent stem wire (gauge 22).

The setting material should be moulded into the container very firmly. It should overlap the brim and stand at least one-and-a-half inches—or more—above the level of the vase (as shown in Fig. 32 on page 89). Alternatively, a rounded mould of Plasticine can be placed in a saucer or ash-tray, or in a shell, or on a porcelain or glass tile (as can be bought in Woolworths, for instance): when well pressed down, this makes a splendid foundation in which to fix many a dried arrangement.

TOOLS

These are simple and few—it is the way they are employed, rather than their number, that produces the result. As in all forms of floral arranging, it is mainly the arranger's fingers that translate into reality the picture in his mind. The dried flower worker would be well advised to keep all the tools of his trade together in a case—thus they are handy for working on an assembly; for packing and transporting; for use in the inevitable repairs from time to time; and for staging arrangements at exhibitions.

Forceps

When working with dried material, a small pair of forceps will be essential. (These are obtainable in most chemists' stores.) With their help the smallest leaf or finest grass or most temperamental seed-capsule can be effectively placed in any position, at any angle, and at any stage of the assembly without disturbing the whole.

A large pair of forceps would be equally useful for work with heavier material.

Secateurs and scissors

These are all-important—the former for harvesting, the latter for assembly. Scissors should be of three kinds:

1. a large pair of **kitchen scissors** for cutting cardboard boxes or cartons and cellophane in preparation for transport;
2. a pair of florists' **stub scissors** with wire-cutting device for harvesting and assembling; and
3. a pair of medium small **fine-bladed scissors** for use during the preserving and assembly stages, for re-shaping frayed leaves and mis-shapen and unattractive flowers, seed-heads, or long flat grasses.

Knives

A small penknife will have many uses at all stages, and a rounded kitchen knife will be effective for cutting and shaping Plasticine, Plastone, and so on.

GLUE

A tube of some good-quality transparent, instant glue such as Uhu is essential, either for small repairs or for fixing some particular item. It is useful, too, for sticking a layer of moss or lichen onto a setting base of Plasticine in a container.

BOSTIK BLU-TACK (formerly Bostik 5) AND STEMFIX ADHESIVE

These re-usable adhesive accessories are quite invaluable. Like Stemfix, Blu-Tack is a form of soft adhesive putty which will fasten any two surfaces so long as they are dry. It will not dry out, is not affected by moisture or extreme temperatures, and can be used over and over again. Dried arrangements are naturally rather lightweight, and its main use is to secure the vase and its contents in the desired position—on table, mantelpiece, bookshelf, or anywhere else. (Cut a small piece (no larger than a big peanut), roll it in the palms of the hands, and put it on the place where the arrangement is to stand. Then gently press the vase down on top of the Blu-Tack "ball" so that the latter becomes flat and invisible; the arrangement will then be secure in its desired position.) Blu-Tack can be safely used on polished or antique furniture, painted woods, and so on, and is undeniably quite invaluable for displaying delicate porcelain. To remove it, pull gently, or just "roll off", and then it is ready, once again, for use.

WIRE AND GUTTA-PERCHA

These materials are dealt with in the section on wiring and binding which appears on pages 84-86. To summarise, however, the dried flower arranger should always have to hand various gauges of stub wire, in convenient lengths; reels of fine wire; and reels of gutta-percha for binding false stems.

ADHESIVE TAPE

Sellotape, or similar adhesive tape, can be most useful and should always be to hand. It can reinforce the wiring at the back of a feeble leaf or spray, and can also make feasible the bending of these to a special angle. It is also effective for binding round the back or base of preserved flowers to prevent petals from falling or becoming displaced, and for securing the setting material, such as Plasticine, at the back of a difficult arrangement.

Fig. 27: this somewhat imposing dried creation was designed recently, to exact measurements, to fill a glass display case at the entrance to a large reception area. Its main object was to back up a feature article on the Rose here depicted, that most evocative and beautiful of flowers, and queen of fragrance (albeit dried for this particular purpose). The arrangement was designed for the pedestal on which it is set and which suits it well, giving plenty of scope for trailing sprays. It stands some seven to eight feet high, and this demanded extra special care in the preparation of the preliminary "mechanics" and fixing a firm base to hold such tall and sweeping material. The roses were preserved in stages over several weeks. Though all red, they were in many different hues, ranging from darkest red through many shades of purple and mauve to palest pink. They were set sparsely at the top, with mingling clusters in the centre, spreading widely to the sides and downwards, and with some towards the back. Trailing sprays of wired flowers of *Helipterum*, and greenery, were added to maintain the balance and to add delicacy. It was an assignment demanding much work, initiative and imagination, as nearly always happens when the arranger is confined to working in a set dimension. The rose's charms are most sweet but inevitably frail, growing and withering as it does in single blessedness, and it was a joy to try to perpetuate something of the beauty of this veritable message from Heaven.

Fig. 28: "mechanics" are essential to a successful assembly.

1.   A pedestal seven and a half inches high on which the arrangements are assembled; an upturned clay flower pot would do perfectly well as a substitute. On this are a pair of florist's stub scissors, a miniature duplicate pair for carrying in the pocket, and a small pair of forceps for making final delicate adjustments.

2.   A reel of stone-coloured Gutta-Percha tape, for binding false wire stems.

3.   A roll of Bostik "Blu-Tack", the re-usable adhesive which is used for securing the arrangement in its chosen position.

4.   A packet of Twist-its, used for tying small bunches of fragile seed-heads, delicate flowers, and so on which are to be hung up to dry. (Twist-its are obtainable from any horticultural sundries-man.)

5.   A roll of *soft* twine for tying up bigger, heavier bunches for drying.

6.   A twist of green-coloured plastic-covered wire; this makes a good light hanging line.

7.   A reel of sellotape which can be used to reinforce the wiring at the back of a feeble leaf, or for binding round the back or base of a flower to prevent the petals from drooping or falling.

8.   A larger pair of forceps for handling heavier dried material.

9.   A pair of fine-bladed scissors for use in reshaping frayed leaves, mis-shapen flowers, and so on, at the grooming stage.

10.   An old garden knife, used for cutting Plasticine, grubbing up moss and harvesting lichen and cutting Oasis or Stemfix blocks.

11.   Reels of fine wire in different gauges for use in fastening false stems.

12.   Bundles of florists' wire in different gauges.

13.   A piece of Plasticine which is used as the setting material (delicate preserved flowers and seed-heads can also be stuck into mounds of this for temporary storage).

14.   Dried hollow plant stalks; these can be reinforced with wire to make false stems with a particularly "natural look" which can be fixed to preserved blooms, leaves and seed-heads.

15.   A packet of Stemfix; this is another kind of re-usable adhesive which is useful for securing a small light arrangement. A piece no bigger than a peanut is all that is required. The adhesive can be removed after use and no mark is left on painted or polished furniture. The process is described in detail on page 81.

16.   A block of green foam-like Stemfix which is very useful for storing delicate material awaiting assembly (as shown in Fig. 24).

17.   A Woolworths' sherry glass, with a double lining of polythene to give it an opaque iridescent appearance and to hide the mechanics within.

18.   A tube of Uhu instant glue which has multiple uses: for attaching a fine wire along the back of a delicate leaf; for lightly coating the outer petals of a drooping flower head; and so on. The tube is lying on a small perspex stand or pedestal which can be used instead of a container; a mound of Plasticine can be set firmly on this stand, and the dried material inserted as usual to make up a different style of arrangement, which gives the appearance of springing directly from the perspex stem.

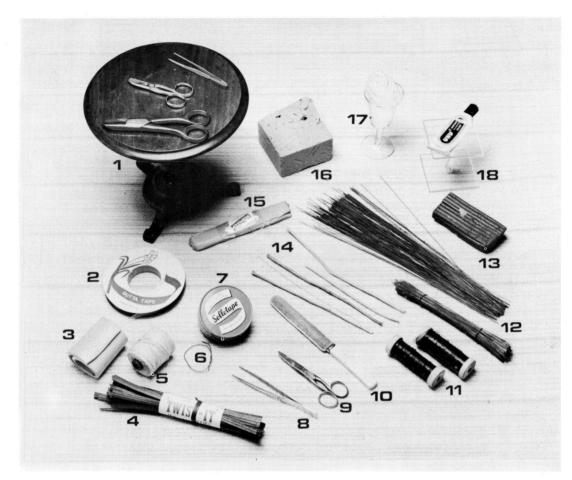

Fig. 28

Lighting

A good working light is essential—in fact, ideally there should be two lights: one with a 200-watt electric light bulb for general assembly, and another, preferably of an Anglepoise type, with a blue daylight bulb, which will greatly assist in selecting and blending colours.

Preparation for Assembly

Before actually starting to arrange, the worker needs to take stock of the material already dried, preserved, and suitably prepared. Careful preparation should have been made at the time of harvesting so that all the material gathered was in prime condition, ready for the preserving processes. When one reaches the stage of preparation for assembly, nothing more than a final "look-over", trim or titivation should be necessary A flower-head may be in need of grooming—a distorted, blemished or ill-placed leaf may need to be removed, or re-shaped yet again with fine-bladed scissors—a small branch or twig may have to be discreetly pruned, a seed-vessel re-varnished—all according to what part they are to play in a particular assembly. Grasses should be looked over and only those of a green hue retained. Mosses should be checked, and insects and clinging leaves removed. Lichens should also be given attention.

Though the idea of "grooming" may sometimes be regarded as merely a florists' term for "bringing up to perfection", its importance cannot be over-estimated and will assuredly prove a supreme asset for the arranger, and perhaps, more important than anything, of lasting value in the final result.

The store needs to be "opened up" and set ready for use, and the work of the arranger will be greatly facilitated if all the material can be viewed, so to speak, at a glance, and is put into some sort of order and sequence for use.

Cartons containing upright seed-heads, fluffy grasses, *Alchemilla mollis*, eryngium, echinops, horse-mint, ballota, molucella, wired helichrysums, and so on, should be grouped ready for immediate use. The same principle applies to open florists' boxes containing material which has been lain flat—such as non-fluffy grasses, varnished corn, pressed ferns, small favourite bits and pieces of all sorts and, of course, the treasured processed flowers waiting to act as special "centrepieces". The delicate, chemically-preserved flower-heads on their false stems are standing ready in their blocks of Stemfix foam (Fig. 24 on page 74).

The heavier items can be brought down from the beam or wire on which they were hanging upside down, and placed ready for use: such things as acanthus, agapanthus seed-heads, the umbellifers—cow parsnip, for example, angelica, fennel, parsley—dock and sorrel and the smaller bunches of rhodanthe, acroclinium, anaphalis, ammobium, phlomis, and many of the silver-leaved plants (artemisias, senecios, *Cineraria maritima*, stachys, santolinas, and so on) which have been loosely dried.

The pressed leaves and ferns should, however, remain *face downwards*, as always, between their respective sheets of blotting paper, thus preventing any possible curling of the leaves before the process of assembly begins.

Wiring and Binding

Various gauges of stub wire, in convenient lengths, should always be to hand in the store; also, reels of fine wire—preferably black, although the finest types of fuse wire seem always to be silver. Stub wire is used for inserting in hollow stalks, to reinforce them; or as a false stem, suitably attached to a leaf, flower or seed-head, being bound to it with fine reel wire and thereafter, if necessary, covered with gutta-percha or other binding material; or for laying along the back of a spray or leaf, again as a reinforcement (any leaf which is weak at the neck can be given a false stem of stub wire, which can be extended a short way up the back of the leaf and fixed along the mid-vein with thin strips of adhesive tape). The slender stems of many grasses, such as *Lagurus ovatus* (Hare's-Tail) should be given false stems, reaching about halfway up, in order to prevent the slightly top-heavy "fluff" from bending over and breaking them.

Fig. 29 shows the author putting a false wire stem on a beautiful tree paeony leaf. Acanthus leaves, already wired, are standing in the sherry glass.

Some flower-heads, such as helichrysums, dahlias, zinnias, roses and gentians, are best wired *before* drying—for during the drying process the flower-stem shrinks and so clings to the wire, right up to the base of the flower. Mr George W. Smith gives the following advice on how to wire helichrysums. "Pick each flower-bud with half an inch of stem and carefully insert a 22-gauge florist's iron wire up the hollow stem. Push this up until it enters the seed-box, just above the neck of the flower. Great care should be taken not to insert the wire so far that it may later project from the centre of the petals, for the flower will continue to develop and open, and would thus display the end of the wire. Never insert a wire with a hooked end through the flower-head, an unsightly method practised by some florists on open flowers. The secret of the process described above is that the juice remaining in the seed-box and stalk causes the iron wire to rust slightly and a very strong union is forged between the flower and the wire. Wires are sold in various lengths—a ten-inch wire is the most useful." Wired helichrysums appear in several of the illustrations.

Fig. 30: the author is wiring a centaurea seed-head. Other dried centaureas and sprigs of dried box are lying flat in the box in the foreground. The assembly on which she is working is shown on the far left.

A special note on the wiring of dried hydrangea heads is given on page 90, and the process is illustrated in Fig. 15 on page 53.

Reels of gutta-percha for binding false stems can be obtained in different colours; the stone shade is perfect for dried material. In fact, the use of such binding for stems is hardly necessary if the assembly is sufficiently full of leaves, grasses and background material to ensure that the wire stems are invisible—and this is particularly applicable to the small type of flower arrangements discussed here. For the large types, binding the false stems will be far more necessary.

To bind, begin at the top of the stalk. Hold the wire and the stalk together just beneath the flower-head with the forefinger and the thumb. Still keeping a firm hold, start winding the gutta-percha from the top with the other hand, and gradually twist it tightly at a downward slanting angle (see Fig. 31 on page 87). As gutta-percha is self-sealing, there is no need to use any adhesive. If, however, another binding material is used, the bottom end should be secured with an adhesive glue.

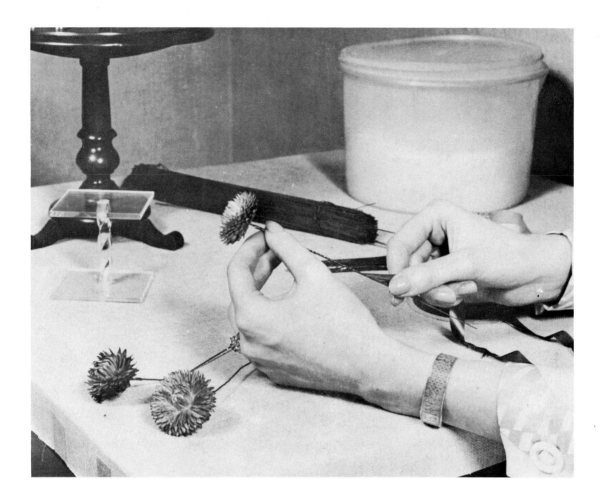

Fig. 31: some flowers, among them helichrysums, should be given false wire stems before preserving. The flower-heads which are shown in the illustration above were each picked with half an inch of the natural stem. A false wire stem is then bound with fine reel wire to the natural stem. In the illustration this false stem is being covered with gutta-percha.

Binding begins at the top of the stalk. The wire and the stalk are held together just beneath the flower-head with fore finger and thumb, and the gutta-percha is wound downwards from the top, being twisted tightly round the false stem at a slanting angle (gutta-percha is self-sealing and there is therefore no need to secure the last twist with an adhesive).

In the background is a bundle of stub wire, and to the right is the circular air-tight container—the "witches' cauldron"—in which the flowers are to be immersed. This is already half full of silica gel crystals; the wired flower heads will be placed carefully inside and completely covered with more crystals. A reel of gutta-percha is visible under the right wrist, and on the far left is a polythene display stand.

The Creative Imagination

As for assembly itself, well, that must finally rest with the arranger. He alone knows what he has in mind—or does he? Indeed, when he sets out, his sense of creativity and imagination may more than likely carry him away—far beyond his original intention—and so often this is how the greatest and most spontaneous success is achieved. Some particular motive inspires—some outstanding specimen demands—some pressing desire impels. It is in his hands to design and create whatever picture he has in mind, and in his artistry will be revealed the final expression of his craft—a craft full of endless possibilities, economic in materials and long-lasting in results—indeed, a craft open to all who are inspired by experiment and phantasy to preserve and enhance the bounteous gifts of Nature.

Notes on Arranging

It will be found, in nearly all instances, that dried material is most attractively assembled "three-dimensionally", unless an "all-round" or "cone" shape is specifically desired.

When arranging dried material, it is best to work with the assembly a little above eye-level—two inches, or less, would do. A pedestal, like the one shown in Fig. 32 and many of the other illustrations, would do excellently; alternatively, a box or some similar stand.

To achieve an easy-flowing line, with no hint or suggestion of stiffness, is perhaps the greatest essential when working with dried material. In order to accomplish this, the highest point in the arrangement should lean slightly—but only fractionally—backwards, whereas the right and left sides should, so to speak, "play it both ways".

Make a start by placing a selection of different leaves to suit the type of arrangement in mind, as shown in Fig. 32 on page 89—the remainder of the leaves can be added later to complete the composition. Then turn to picking out items for the "central top" point—tapering larkspur, a delphinium bloom, a spray of ballota, a spike of dock seed-head, or salvia. Repeat these additions at irregular intervals throughout the arrangement, reserving the largest blooms or seed-heads for the "central base". At this stage it will be necessary to choose material for "insetting": anaphalis, for example, achillea, hydrangea, or varnished clematis seed-heads.

After the main seed-heads and flowers have been placed, the arranger can turn to the addition of grasses, both fluffy and non-fluffy, and delicate sprays of nipplewort (which features frequently in the illustrations in this book), salvia seed-heads, grevillea leaves, maiden-hair fern and other similar materials, which will ensure a soft outline and marry up the "central top" with the "back"—so essential for soft-flowing side-effects.

When placing seed-heads and flowers, attention should be given to those which catch the light, so that they can be suitably distributed; and some of the darker items look well when set back in order to allow the more delicate subjects to protrude. A soft, uneven outline, especially towards the front and sides, must always be the aim in "three-dimensional" arrangements.

Fig. 32: a view of the work-table with the first stages of assembly shown on the pedestal at the back. Notice how the sherry glass has been filled with Plasticine which stands a good inch and a half above the brim. This is the setting material in which the first four leaves have already been placed; a maple leaf on either side, a drooping spray in front and a spear of fern arching up and away at the back. Notice too the good light, and the tin of clear varnish used for varnishing seed-heads of clematis, rose bay and so on. The tools, "mechanics", display stands and other essentials are neatly arranged and ready to hand.

Hydrangea flower-heads should nearly always be split up into smaller segments and given wire stems (start wiring at the top by hooking the stub wire over and through the delicate flower-head bracts, as shown in Fig. 15 on page 53, and binding in place with fine reel wire). Such pieces are invaluable for "in-filling" low in the front of the arrangement and partially round the sides.

Clematis seed-heads, both fluffy and stiffly varnished, need to be placed so that the smaller heads are midway up in the arrangement and out at the sides, and the larger ones set low down in front. A mixture of both types, side by side, is most effective. This can be seen in Fig. 7 on page 37, for example.

When dried flower spikes, like delphinium, larkspur, ballota, molucella, salvia, and so on, are too long, they can be cut in half, or even into small pieces, and trimmed, re-shaped and wired on false stems (a special section on wiring and binding appears on pages 84-86). They can all be used for different assemblies, so making the most of material in short supply. The top pieces, with their tapering points, will look well high up in the arrangement, while the lower portions, with their dense growth, will be useful for placing low.

When the front is completed, turn the arrangement right round and work on the back, using up small ends left over—sprigs of conifer and box, and odd leaves of laurel, rhododendron, and so on, are ideal material with which to create a fairly flat, protective back. The completed back should slant slightly outwards (this has been found helpful). Nothing should protrude too far, or the assembly will be too bulky and it will be difficult to stand it safely on a mantel-piece or narrow shelf.

(After the arrangement is completed, all unused leaves should be put back in their respective sheets of blotting paper, face downwards. One can never have too many leaves, and it is therefore important to conserve one's stock.)

The Value of Leaves

Working with dried material, one is more limited as regards bright colours and supple texture than when handling a choice of fresh flowers and leaves. It is therefore necessary to rely on a far greater interplay between different forms and varieties of leaves, such as sprays of green rhododendron and dark brown Portuguese laurel—both inclined to be somewhat stiff (but invaluable for a secure background)—and the more supple and dangly, light-catching, green-grey eucalyptus sprays (spraying out to mid-left in the frontispiece), the delicately veined beech in varying colours of brown or *Elæagnus ebbingei* with their olive-green surfaces and oyster-white underneaths—these are semi-stiff but none the less pliable if gently moulded between finger and thumb, and nearly always have prettily curved short stems.

Many leaves which are white, oyster or silver underneath look well if arranged back to front: celmisia, for example, *Viburnum rhytidophyllum*, whitebeam, *Elæagnus ebbingei*, and the like. Celmisia leaves were inserted thus in Fig. 26 on page 77 to create a silvery effect.

Then there are numerous, and quite invaluable, toothed and segmented leaves, such as paeonies, both tree and herbaceous (the former with beautiful coloured markings), bramble—as mentioned on page 31—geranium, *Anemone pulsatilla*, clematis, sycamore, maple, especially *Acer palmatum*, and an infinite number of others.

In dried arrangements the plentiful use of a wide variety of leaves, not all of the same species, is essential—for not only do they give depth and a sense of greenness, and therefore a more "live" impression, but they protect each other against curling and cracking. They create a basic sense of muted tints which, with the addition of ferns, seed-heads, grasses and flowers, may well complete the harmony of the arrangement.

Another important point for the worker to bear in mind throughout the process of arranging is that the utilitarian devices, or "mechanics" (described on pages 78-81), must be discreetly and unobtrusively hidden. This can best be done by the strategic placing of leaves at different angles and at varying heights and sometimes in groups, according to the type of design and what material is available. At this stage in the assembly the use of small forceps will be of great assistance in positioning the leaves.

Many of the short-stalked leaves will require false stems of stub wire. Leaves which may be slightly limp or weak at the neck can be supported by carrying the stub wire a short way up the back of the leaf—this can be fixed along the central vein with thin strips of sellotape or glue.

When arranging sprays of leaves such as laurel, elaeagnus, box, ivy, conifers, whitebeam, *Viburnum rhytidophyllum*, and so on, remove superfluous leaves, and, after wiring, use them elsewhere in the arrangement, or retain them for future use. Such pieces are particularly useful for drooping low in the container, as in Fig. 8 on page 40, or filling in at the back of the arrangement.

Mixed Fresh and Dried Material

It is possible in an emergency, when fresh flowers are in short supply, to add a particularly nice-looking dried bloom to a vase of fresh greenery in water. The wire or dried stem will withstand being immersed in water for a considerable time. The best dried flowers to use for this purpose are any of the everlastings, such as helichrysums, rhodanthe, acrocliniums and others, and also any appropriate seed-heads or wired leaves. A favourite dried bloom or seed-head can be set in an arrangement of fresh leaves or a collection of pickings from a walk round the garden, along the hedgerow or by the waterside—the fresh leaves will ultimately shrivel, but the preserved flower may well go on to fulfil other roles, enhancing many more assemblies with its grace and colour. This practice should, nevertheless, only be resorted to when real flowers are at a premium, as a means to tide over a crisis. It is not to be advocated for regular use as when mixed neither fresh nor dried material do justice to each other. Fig. 19 on page 65 shows an arrangement of mixed fresh and dried material, which was assembled early one February in a London flat.

Other Forms of Dried Material Assembly

To treat this fascinating subject in all the detail it deserves would almost need another book. Much of the craft emanates from ancient folklore and long-ago traditions. There is, for instance, the ancient Christmas symbol of a globe, or crown, written about by Laurence Whistler in his *The English Festivals;* and Constance Spry describes the Kissing Bough or Branch in her *Garden Notebook* and *Winter and Spring Flowers*. More recently, we have had a wealth of information and ideas, with illustrations, in George W. Smith's *Flower Arrangements and Their Setting*. He shows examples of wall plaques, swags, panels, garlands, festoons, cone-shaped trees, and—that most delightful custom—door bows. Furthermore, there is a growing interest in creating flower pictures—some very beautiful—with flowers which are pressed or appliqué on backgrounds of silk or velvet; another revival of past ages.

Arrangements in Miniature

Though this might appear, at first sight, as a subject in "minuscule", the dried flower arranger needs to give it much thought. A miniature arrangement is not just "a few flowers" or "a posy" hurriedly collected and put together to take to someone as a "token".

Like so much in this modern age, the flower world is visibly changing very rapidly, and successful marketing requires acute vigilance, as much for a miniature as for a grand-scale arrangement. The would-be arranger, for instance, be he engaged with fresh or with dried material, must forever bear in mind the frustrating modern practice of forcing or retarding flowers, to coincide with lucrative seasonal demands. From both aspects—fresh or dried— it can be hazardous for the purchaser and devastating for the arranger. For the dried material arranger, however, the matter should not present too many difficulties, because he is handling delicate material such as dried species, seed-heads, fine grasses, and specially selected pressed leaves— preferably obtained from gardens direct.

For preservation and assembly, the theories already described apply, but with the whole procedure scaled down to size: appropriately selected, delicate, miniature material in suitable containers. The arranger should bear in mind the final object to be achieved. If the arrangement is for a bedside in hospital, it may have to survive some weeks in varying positions, and it should always contain the most enchanting material possible—maybe delicate, but durable. If, on the other hand; the arranger is composing "a token gesture" for some particular occasion, such as "Thank You" or "Good Wishes", the material used may vary more widely in character and the arrangement remain for many seasons, a happy memory.

Dried arrangements are becoming increasingly popular, and it will pay the collector to preserve tiny items in his store. Because of their small size and very personal character, the individual items should be specially selected and painstakingly assembled. There is no doubt that such "miniatures" can give pleasure to many people.

Arrangement in Churches

The words of Constance Spry heading this chapter on Assembly are perhaps more profoundly applicable to this section than to anywhere else in the book. It is indeed not enough only to love flowers—to preserve them without blemish—to arrange them for setting in places of worship— no indeed, they must also be studied and understood, sensitively selected, carefully handled, their suitability for being placed in some particular part of the church—at the foot of some special shrine, in a corner of a chapel—most patiently assessed, so that they may evoke thoughts in keeping with a theme, a fantasy, a liturgical occasion.

However irksome it may be, we must become realistic and face the fact that times have changed—and are continuing to do so rapidly—and that therefore new methods must be brought into play. Fortunately for the dried flower arranger this should be not only easy but stirring. After all, are we not for ever reminded of the mystical significance of worship, dating back to long before Christian times, with man's interpretation of reverence, meditation, penance, adoration, and exultation, made visible in stained glass windows, carvings, stonework, in frescoes and mosaics, in drapings and vestments? Yes, modern trends are with us—changing communities, scattered parishes, and the inevitable "weekend", which seems to have a habit of being, not uncommonly, stretchable! No longer is it easy to maintain the rota of fresh flower arrangers, erstwhile unchanging—especially not in city parishes. Hence, a special form of dried arrangement has developed, to an increasing degree, and this, by force of circumstances, is producing for the perceptive dried flower arranger an absorbing new challenge.

To begin with, adapting dried assemblies appropriately to embellish and enhance places of worship demands special consideration, infinite thought. At first, this project could well be awe-inspiring to the would-be arranger, but with experience, derived from infinite study, intuition can surmount a multitude of hurdles, so long as the liturgy itself, and the objects of the different services, are first understood. To ensure this, the arranger should become conversant with the Church's calendar, its regular and special services, and should, at all times, seek and observe directions from the parish priest and clergy.

Another point of importance in Church work is to ensure that only the best flowers and foliage material are used. These must be bought direct from the market and examined, as to the perfection of their condition, before purchase: no forced or retarded material (so constantly, now, on sale) will undergo dried preservation with success. This is of vital consideration when it is realised that satisfactory dried arrangements in churches may and do survive in attractive condition for many seasons.

As in all flower work, the arranger has to learn to overcome the major disadvantages of being precluded from arranging *in situ* (as with fresh flowers). Consequently, there is the complication of transport: preserved flowers do not pack well individually, and pressed leaves tend to be brittle. It is therefore, essential for the dried arrangement to be assembled, at least in its greater part, at home or in the studio. The inevitable last-minute wiring takes a long time, and the re-siting of pressed foliage tends to create more debris than may conveniently be handled during assembly in church. Luckily, the solution lies in the use of properly constructed, wrought iron, florists' pedestals, which not only unscrew midway down the shaft, thus facilitating transport, but are also well in keeping with their church destination. These pedestals, too, being movable, lend themselves appropriately to church use for seasonal occasions—as, for instance, Lent and Holy Week, when there are no flowers in church—and may also be moved to make way for fresh flower assemblies when weddings, funerals, and so on, are being held, or when flower festivals are staged.

Lastly, the dried flower arranger may, in spite of his exacting task, restrictions, and challenging demands, take heart. Let him relax and reflect: after all, is he not simply following in the footsteps of the great masters of painting who, when short of some particularly enchanting addition to fill a demanding gap in a composition, had recourse to their "store", and portrayed prize blooms whose flowering dates might in sober reality range over many months. Some artists' licence may not come amiss!

CONTAINERS

Introduction

So far as containers for the type of dried arrangements discussed in this book are concerned, the choice is comparatively easy: the simpler the better.

The predominant feature of this type and style of arrangement is in essence traditional, delicate, light—indeed, it is, one hopes, an expression of nature in its most true and captivating form. No gimmicks, no artificial colour, no unnatural aids play any part in the theme. Rather is it to be recognised as an essay in bringing together, in simple and appropriate assembly, the manifold beauties of nature, culled with appreciation and diligence throughout the seasons. Fritillary and grape hyacinth seed-heads in the spring—the columbine and scilla seed-heads next—the bent and timothy grasses in early summer—the paeony, maple and viburnum leaves—and so many others as the season grows—until finally, by September and October, the store is almost complete (except for the late leaves, hydrangea heads and the like); and at this stage in the sequence, the question of an appropriate container in which to arrange them becomes paramount.

Whereas the fresh flower arranger works *in situ*, the dried flower arranger should have the pedestal, the container, the mechanics, tools, and accessories all ready, close to the dried material, in a studio-like manner. The dried material worker has the immense advantage of being able to draw from a whole year's harvest at one time, and if the store has been carefully and imaginatively opened up and the contents set out for viewing, selection will be much easier and quicker.

Suggested Containers

With small delicate arrangements, generally not larger than nineteen inches high and eleven inches broad, a champagne, sherry or hock glass is ideal (as in Fig. 13 on page 48)—or a similar size china vase (plain white, soft yellow, dark olive green). So too, are alabaster, soapstone or lead vases, a small tazza, a cornucopia, a cherub holding a shallow bowl, a small candlestick—

any of these are apt and charming containers. Vases of over-heavy design or with gaudy decoration must at all costs be avoided—the muted hues of dried material are best against an unobtrusive background. Owing to its rather brittle nature, dried plant tissue will last longer and look better in a container on a "stem" (as, for instance, the container in Fig. 35 on page 89). This gives scope for a more natural drooping of leaves, grasses and flowers over the rim. Equally, a flat arrangement using an ash-tray, saucer, butter-dish, mirror or tile (which can be bought at Woolworths), can make a delightful variation, with, say, a clump of gentians or other small flowers, leaves and ferns, set in moss, or lichen-covered Plasticine. When using a wine-glass container (not too opaque) a charming iridescent effect can be obtained by lining the glass with a double thickness of clear cellophane before putting in silver-sand (if used) and the Plasticine. This also serves to hide the "mechanics" within.

There are, of course, endless ways of arranging dried plant material in many types of containers. So much depends on personal taste. The arranger has a splendid excuse for browsing among antique shops, in "reject" china and glass stores, at bric-a-brac stalls and country sales—the choice is wide, the scope enormous, and excitement can be intense. One firm in particular, whose designs are highly pleasing and suitable for dried arrangements, is Elaine Goddard Ltd (whose address is given on page 154).

Display Stands

For exhibition purposes, whether the arrangement is for decoration, competition, or sale, a stand on which to display the assembly is really indispensable. Candlesticks of wood, metal, porcelain or glass can make very effective stands, with a flat painted platform fixed over the candle-socket. Similarly, trade display stands, of composition, foam, or perspex, such as those to be found in shop display fitters', are useful. Messrs Anjay Displays Ltd have a wonderful selection of display material in perspex and mirrored glass. If all these are lacking, then upturned painted flower-pots or paper-covered boxes can prove helpful. For large arrangements, pedestals and torchères are obvious choices.

Positioning the Arrangement

As the type of arrangements with which this book is mostly concerned are not cumbersome, they can be moved easily from place to place—for instance, on the mantelpiece (so long as it is cool there), at the corner of a bookshelf, on top of the television set, on a writing table, and not infrequently on the spare bedroom dressing-table. Because of their "three-dimensional" design, they are best placed against a background of walls, pictures or books. The all-round type of arrangement does not make an effective centre-piece for a dining-room table as it can look over-stiff. Blu-tack, described on page 81, is most useful in positioning arrangements.

All dried arrangements look their best when viewed from afar, with the light above, below or in front of them—never behind.

PACKING

Introduction

One of the many assets of the small-scale (and not so small) dried arrangement is that with reasonable precautions it can be packed for personal—but never postal—transport. It is quite possible to pack a rather large dried arrangement, or a collection of several small ones, so that they can travel many miles—indeed from one country to another—as long as the package is personally supervised during transit. This applies alike to a single individual gift or sale arrangement or to a collection of assemblies intended for exhibition, either for competition or sale—or for any other purpose. Furthermore, it is possible to arrange for satisfactory transport by rail (and why not by sea or air?) so long as personal despatch and collection is assured and precautionary instructions clearly displayed on the package. Responsibility for successful transport lies primarily with the packer, and so long as the intervening journey proves smooth and without too many hazards, there is no reason why many arrangements should not continue their role in surroundings far from the original habitat.

Experience has shown that it is possible, with the necessary assistance, to transport by car hundreds of very fragile arrangements—of all shapes and forms—from the studio to their destination and, in the case of exhibition, to bring them home again intact.

The following points should be carefully borne in mind—no doubt, in course of experience, others will arise.

Principles of Successful Packing

MODE OF PACKING

This is of the utmost importance. It will be up to the packer to decide whether the arrangement should travel in an upright position, or lying, suitably supported, on its back. For arrangements which are cone- or circular-shaped—or indeed, "three-dimensional" in shape—the upright position is essential. For all others, no matter how tall, or delicate, lying flat is preferable.

TYPES OF PACKING CASE

Packing cases should be, roughly, of two types:

1. **flat**: a strong, flat florist's box or dress-box, the base suitably reinforced with strengthening strips of flat cardboard, secured by adhesive tape, or sellotape, and with sides which have also been reinforced where necessary; or

2. **upright**: a deep, rectangular carton, such as used by wine merchants or grocers; a large egg-container; a chemists' packing case; or a large wooden slatted produce-packing basket.

In both instances, the packing case can, if necessary, be suitably re-constructed in shape to meet requirements. This is particularly necessary with very tall arrangements, which should always be packed flat. Here, it may be necessary to use two, or even four, long florists' boxes, with the edges flattened, to procure the necessary length or width. The whole can be strengthened with extra strips of cardboard, made secure by use of adhesive tape or Sellotape.

PROTECTIVE PADDING

The safe transport of a fragile arrangement, particularly one including delicate, arching grasses, and drooping sprays, depends almost wholly on extremely careful padding and support against movement and vibration. It is essential to use the thinnest and least expensive type of tissue paper (the kind that barely crinkles when compressed). Be lavish in its use.

Packing

First of all, line the box plentifully throughout with tissue paper, and arrange surplus sheets so as to hang over the outer edges (these will subsequently be folded gently around the arrangement). If packing *flat*, make a "nest" with smooth tissue paper padding, in which to put the arrangement. A layer of tissue paper should be swathed carefully round the vase to protect any material which hangs over the rim, and the whole arrangement should then be laid on its back in the already prepared "nest". Next, fill in all side spaces carefully and lightly, with crumpled tissue paper, leaving the top and uppermost end open to view. Fold or roll in the overlapping sheets of tissue round the inside of the edges, and secure with Sellotape. Finally, cover the entire top with a light sheet of cellophane or polythene, sufficiently crumpled and loose to allow for it not to squash any protruding grass, fern, or seed-head. Fix this sheet to the outside of the box or carton with Sellotape, thus providing complete protection against wind or rain. Small thin bamboo canes or stout twigs can be attached to the four corners of the carton to support the cellophane. An alternative is to surround the arrangement loosely with layers of tissue paper in the form of a circular tent, and clip the paper together, at intervals, with a "Bambi" type stapler, as used by florists. The arrangement should then be carried *upright*.

Spare Parts

It is always advisable to carry a few previously prepared surplus grasses, leaves, and so on, in case of any breakages during transit. Spare reel wire and stub wire, Plasticine, sellotape and scissors should be included as well.

Part Two
FLORILEGIUM

All the names I know . . .
* Gardener's Garters, Shepherd's Purse,*
Bachelor's Buttons, Lady's Smock,
* And the Lady Hollyhock.*

ROBERT LOUIS STEVENSON: *The Flowers*

Author's Note

The following list of trees, shrubs and plants aims at being a guide to the dried material collector; it is by no means exhaustive, and could be added to considerably.

No specific mention has generally been made of the colour of the flowers or of their harvesting times, since the genera described have in many cases many species and varieties worthy of attention. Then, too, some are recommended for their leaves, others for their flowers or seed-heads—nearly all of which have been referred to in Part One.

Editor's Note

In some cases in the following list, the whole genus is referred to; where this happens, the heading gives first the generic name, then the family name, and then the vernacular name, if any, for the genus. In other cases, one particular species is described; if so, the name of the species is inserted after the generic name, and the vernacular name for the species follows the family name.

ACANTHUS——*Acanthaceæ*——BEAR'S BREECH

> *Good for members out of yointe and burninge if it be layd upon the diseased places.*
> *. . . It is wonderful good for burstinges and places drawen together . . . . Plinye*
> *sayeth also that thys herbe is good for the goute.*

William Turner: Herball

A. mollis latifolius: this late-flowering garden plant from Italy with long, shiny, arching and undulating, deeply lobed and classically architectural leaves, may have been the source of inspiration for that brain-child of the ancient Greeks, the capital of the Corinthian column.

These leaves should be greatly treasured for pressing—especially the smaller ones. The towering spikes of pink-white flowers, too, can easily be preserved if dried hanging upside down, and are impressive in large arrangements. Keep a good supply of both in the store. A sweeping arc of acanthus, hung from a rafter to dry, appears in the illustration of the granary on page 61 (Fig. 18).

Acanthus species are found growing in the Mediterranean regions of Asia and Africa, and in Abyssinia, and are of value to collectors as experimental material.

In 1200 A.D., Alexander Neckam listed acanthus among the plants which ought to be grown in a "good" garden; but the first English herbalist to describe acanthus in detail was the Tudor botanist, William Turner. It was, he said, "perfitlye knowen in all countries". He described the characteristic deep-cut leaves; added, "The hole herbe is very slymy and full of slippery iuyce"; and referred to the opinions of Dioscorides. There is no doubt that he had first-hand knowledge of the plant—and not merely from his travels in Europe—for he declared, "This herbe growes plenteouslye in my Lordes gardine at Sion."

But one of the earliest written references to acanthus comes long before this, in the celebrated treatise *De architectura*, written by the Roman architect Vitruvius. In this Vitruvius described how another famous architect, Callimachus, set a basket of flowers on his daughter's grave, weighed down with a tile to keep the wind from blowing it away. When next he visited the grave, he found that an acanthus had grown up round the basket, and this so took his fancy that he decided to introduce the leaf into his building designs.

This may, too, explain the use of acanthus in the Language of Flowers to signify the fine arts and artifice.

ACER——*Aceraceæ*——MAPLE

The sweet clothing of the maple tree.

John Clare: *The Maple Tree*

This tribe of trees and shrubs is vast, nearly all of them deciduous, with those most engaging leaves, almost always palmately lobed and sometimes deeply cut, many of which colour so brilliantly as the year goes by. They are nearly always clean, fresh, colourful, and add a lightness and gaiety wherever they are grown, with their tassel-like flowers and seed-head keys.

A. *Pseudoplatanus* (the native British Sycamore) and *A. campestre* (the Wild Field Maple) are happily with us everywhere; the collector of leaves and seed-heads will not have far to look. What a wonderful harvest there is to be gathered. Among the small garden trees are *A. Negundo variegatum* (the multi-coloured Box Elder from North America) and the beautiful *A. griseum* (the Paperbark Maple from China) with its trifoliate autumn-tinted leaves—and then the outstanding collection of Japanese maples, with a picturesque crooked way of growing, such as *A. palmatum atropurpureum*, *A. p. dissectum* and *A. p. Osakazuki* and a host of other beauties—all with autumn leaves exquisite in form and colour. These must be greatly treasured for pressing and storing—indeed, there can never be enough of them. Gay, elegant maple leaves appear in the assembly illustrated on page 45.

ACHILLEA——*Compositæ*——YARROW

The leaves of Yarrow doth close up woundes and keepeth them from inflammation or fiery swelling . . . Most men say, that the leaves chewed, and especially greene, are a remedie for the toothach.

John Gerard: *Herball*

A large genus with many wild and garden species very useful to the dried flower arranger.

A. *filipendulina*, syn. *A. Eupatorium* (the Fernleaf Yarrow from the Caucasus) and its greyish-leaved hybrid "Moonshine" with sulphur flowers, are acknowledged good herbaceous border plants. So also is *A. clypeolata*, with silver-green foliage and beautiful yellow flowers. And again, the German hybrid "Flowers of Sulphur" in soft yellow, and *A. Millefolium* "Cerise Queen" and "Fire King" with flower-heads in bright cerise and deep red respectively. A. *Ptarmica* (the garden Sneezewort) has varieties such as "Pearl" and "Perry White", suitable for the dried collector. In wild form, *A. Millefolium*, with white or pink flowers, and the white *A. Ptarmica* are most attractive and well worth looking for. Harvest all varieties when the flower-heads are still young and dry, and hang them with heads downwards until they are fairly stiff and dry to the tips; then stand loosely upright in a container without water.

Yarrow has been cultivated in Britain for hundreds of years. Gerard describes it, and so does Parkinson—"It is called of some Nose-bleede from making the nose bleed, if it be put into it, but assuredly it will stay the bleeding of it." R. C. A. Prior mentions another old tradition connected with this nickname: an English girl would test her lover's fidelity by tickling her own nose with a sprig of yarrow; if he was still faithful to her, then her nose would bleed. *A. Ptarmica* has a similar old-fashioned name—Sneezewort. But yarrow's principal use was, as Parkinson indicates, to staunch bleeding. Alice Coats, in *Flowers and their Histories*, mentions another country tradition: the growing of yarrow in churchyards as a reproach to the dead "who need never have come there if they had taken their yarrow broth faithfully every day".

ACTINIDIA——*Dilleniaceæ*

The beautiful climbing shrub from Japan and Manchuria and China, *A. Kolomikta* (the Kolomikta Vine), is worth planting in a warm sunny sheltered place, where it will climb by hooking itself to arbours and poles with its petioles. Its main interest for the collector is its tri-coloured leaves, variegated with pink and white, occurring only on wholly mature specimens. Although experiments in pressing these have not yet been carried out, some interesting results may be expected, so long as leaves in prime condition are used. For future experiment, it might be well worth-while taking a good look at other members of this genus—for instance, *A. arguta*, a vigorous climbing specimen from Korea (known as Tara Vine) which has long thin leaves, and *A. polygama* (the Silver Vine) with white and yellow variegated leaves, bronze-tinted when unfolding.

ADIANTUM——*Polypodiaceæ*——MAIDENHAIR FERN

What would the flower arranger do, whether handling fresh or dried material, without this quite superb tribe of ferns in all its many forms, so many with breath-taking lacy filigree of leaves, and all, whether green-house or hardy, so easily preserved, either by glycerine treatment (pages 63-66) or by pressing dry.

A. *venustum* from the Himalayas grows happily in our rock gardens or borders, so long as it is not planted too deeply. The native British wild form, *A. Capillus-Veneris*, may be found growing in sheltered spots on rocks or cliffs in coastal regions of south and north-west England, south Wales, and west Ireland. The genus has many species growing all over the world, whose many tender forms should be sought for and preserved by the collector. The fronds of the larger varieties can be separated and wired singly for particular requirements. Dried adiantum fern can be found on the market, although it is somewhat difficult to come by in its natural state—the bleached form is also most attractive.

In the Language of Flowers it means sincerity.

AGAPANTHUS——*A. Africanus*, syn. *A. umbellatus*——*Liliaceæ*——BLUE AFRICAN
LILY, LILY OF THE NILE

The terminal umbels of the seed-heads of this tender bulbous plant with its beautiful blue flowers, so often seen in terrace or patio tubs, are a great asset for the collector; and the smaller hardy variety, such as the Headbourne hybrids, are useful for the store. As they are autumn-flowering it will be well into the late "back-end" of the year before the seed-heads can be harvested. Their somewhat hollow, succulent stems take some weeks to dry. They are best dried upright with plenty of space between their lovely heads, and can be varnished, if desired.

AGROSTEMMA——*Caryophyllaceæ*

A genus of two species, hardy annual or biennial, whose habitat is Europe and Asia. They do not seem to be very widely known, in spite of their attractive qualities, but they are definitely of value to the dried material worker.

Messrs Thompson & Morgan's seed catalogues list *A. Githago* "Milas" and *A. G.* "Purple Queen". They form a pretty lilac-flowered group in the summer garden and should not be harvested till the flowers are over. The stalks and seed-heads dry quickly and are greatly improved by being dipped into the "drainpipe" varnish container (described on page 66) and then laid out flat to dry on newspaper and turned periodically to prevent sticking. When preserved, the seed-heads make charming delicate and durable additions, especially to small arrangements, and can be used for "outlining", for projecting from the centre, or for drooping over the brim of the container.

The wild form, *A. Githago*, syn. *Lychnis Githago* (the beautiful Corn Cockle of the corn-fields) is alas becoming more rare. Its delicate beauty is worth searching for, as indeed are its leaves and seed-heads with their variegated markings.

ALCHEMILLA——*A. Mollis*——*Rosaceæ*——LADY'S MANTLE

A. Mollis from Asia Minor is a true gardener's delight—easy to grow, easy to propagate, with great ground-cover possibilities and its own unique charm, and frequently displaying on its beautiful kidney-shaped leaves dewdrops which shimmer like quicksilver in the sunshine. Equally fascinating, too, are its flowers with lime-green calyx and no true petals. The garden, fresh flower arrangement, or dried counterpart, are all enhanced by this enchanting out-of-this-world lime-green treasure.

Harvest it in early summer before the rains turn it brown. It is easily preserved by drying loosely upright in a bucket, carton or similar container, which must, of course, be dry.

In the Middle Ages the dewdrops which characteristically gather on its leaves were carefully collected by alchemists (hence its generic name) for use in their experiments to create the Philosophers' Stone, which would, they believed, turn base metal into gold.

ALLIUM——*Liliaceæ*

> *With figge leaves and cummin it is laide on against the bitings of the mouse, called*
> *in English a Shrew.*

William Turner: Herball

This is a vast genus—mostly bulbous herbs, very strong-smelling (not surprising when one reflects that chives, leeks and onions are all cousins).

The ornamental garlics are much prized by the flower arranger. The most attractive and suitable one for dried work is perhaps *A. Moly* with its bright yellow umbels of flowers. If picked in full bloom in midsummer and dried either upright or lying flat in an open box, it provides a charming light cluster of flower-heads of infinite value as centrepiece material in dried arrangements. The larger alliums, such as *A. albopilosum*, syn. *A. Christophii*, produce fascinating and unique star-like rounded spikes which, if pulled apart, are enchanting for small arrangements. Other garden alliums are also worth collecting because of their lasting qualities.

Of all the alliums, *A. Moly* is definitely the star turn—known as the Golden Garlic, it has featured in Britain for several hundred years and was for centuries used in medicinal, and indeed magical, potions. William Turner found a dozen uses for it, shrew bites apart. It was excellent, he said, for those "ieopardies that may come of changing of waters or countrees"—perhaps he had firsthand experience of this, on his travels; it was good for "the bitinges of mad or wood beastes"; it cleared the voice; it could be applied to help luckless sufferers from toothache.

The common name "moly" shows the high esteem in which the Golden Garlic was held, for in Greek legend this was the name of the powerful magic herb which Hermes gave Odysseus to protect him against the spells of the witch Circe. "Here is my moly of much fame, in magics often used," wrote Michael Drayton, the Elizabethan poet; and Edmund Spenser knew it too—"And sweet is Moly, but his root is ill." There are indeed those who dislike the smell and flavour—so be it—but one man's meat is another's poison, and the dried flower arranger should cash in on every possibility at all times.

ALSTRŒMERIA——*Amaryllidaceæ*——PERUVIAN LILY

The *A. Ligtu* hybrids from Chile, which give such superb colour to the herbaceous or shrub border, produce most splendid seed-heads for dried arrangements. There are many other varieties of this rather temperamental fleshy-rooted tribe, with flowers in loose umbels, mostly grown under glass.

It may be well worth-while the collector watching for good seed-heads. Should the flower-heads dry unevenly, the individual seed-pods can be harvested, varnished, and given wire stems. Alstroemeria is the only garden plant which wears its leaves upside down—the leaf-stalks curl so that the undersides of the leaves are displayed; but the dried collector need not worry about this, since he should be watching only for the seed-heads.

ALTHÆA——*Malvaceæ*——HOLLYHOCK

Marrish mallow sodden in wine or mede or brused and layde on by it selfe is good for woundes, for hard kirnels, swellinges and wennes, for ye burning and swelling behind ye eares.

William Turner: *Herball*

Two of the many species of the *Althæa* (Mallow) genus bear the name "hollyhock". They are *A. rosea*, syn. *A. chinensis*, the original hollyhock from China, and *A. ficifolia* (the Figleaf or Antwerp Hollyhock), a native of Europe. Thomas Hyll described the stately garden hollyhock in his *The Proffitable Arte of Gardening*, published in 1574—"Like in beautie unto the rose, although not so strong of savour, and sweete of smell . . . And the floure doth both open at the full appearance of the Sunne and shutteth again at the setting of the Sunne"—but it really came into its own handsome self in the seventeenth century when architects took over garden layouts from botanists, and raised terraces leading down to parterres became highlights in the newly conceived plan. It was then, in company with the lily, love-lies-bleeding, marigold, carnation and crown imperial, that the hollyhock took its ornamental place. Parkinson described it in his *Paradisus:* they "yield out their flowers like Roses on their tall branches, like Trees, to sute you with flowers, when almost you have no other to grace out your Garden." From then on it has happily graced whatever position it has been chosen to occupy, whether alongside a grand terrace or against a homely kitchen garden wall.

The enchanting flowers—preferably the double ones—and later their seed-heads should be preserved and dried respectively. But with hollyhocks, as with delphiniums and other garden favourites, two interests are in opposition to one another: should they be left to fill the garden with colour or plucked for winter's dried arrangements? Luckily, hollyhock flowers are profuse, and a subtle thieving here and there should hardly be noticed! The nurserymen's modern *A. rosea* "Begonia-flowered", "Chater's Double Mixed", and the new "Powder Puffs" and "Silver Puffs"—all give magnificent double blooms, and a brilliant colour display, so everyone should be content.

Finally for good measure it should be recorded that in the Language of Flowers the hollyhock signifies fecundity.

ANAPHALIS——*Compositæ*

The pretty-foliaged, starry-white everlasting, *A. margaritacea*, is invaluable when cream or off-white is needed in a large and rather spreading arrangement. These blooms are, too, perfect for "insetting" in front and are often used in dried flower assemblies. The Himalayan *A. triplinervis* is most popular, and rightly so—it has pearl-white flowers and long leaves (white and woolly beneath, delightfully cobwebby above), and is exquisite and very long-lasting. However, *A. yedœnsis*, with its more compact flower-heads, could be equally attractive. There are other varieties as well which might be worth trying.

Gather the flowers before they become full-blown, and hang them upside down to dry. Do not strip off the foliage, except any damaged leaves, as this dries prettily and enhances the final effect. Anaphalis should be grown and preserved in quantity as it lasts usefully for years.

The commercial *Gnaphalium* (Cudweed) sold on the market is found across North America, Europe and Asia.

The wild everlasting should be looked for in pastures and fields—flowering in August; as also its relative, the wild cudweed, in its varying species.

ANEMONE——*Ranunculaceæ*

The Anemones likewise or Windeflowers are so full of variety and so dainty, pleasant and so delightsome.

John Parkinson: *Paradisus*

These very attractive perennials flowering in the garden during spring, summer and autumn, and flowering wild during the early summer, offer some most beautiful, much-divided, fern-like basal leaves, which dry perfectly between sheets of blotting paper.

A. Pulsatilla, syn. *A. alpina*, was called the Pasque Flower by Gerard because it flowers at Paschaltide. Another old-fashioned name for it is the Flaw Flower—from a "flaw", or small ruffling gust of wind. It is a native of Great Britain, and has been cultivated in cottage gardens for several hundred years. "They serve only for the adorning of gardens and garlands," wrote Gerard, "being flowers of great beautie." Alice Coats quotes Miss Sackville West's description in *The Garden*:

Lavender petals sheathed in silver floss
Soft as the suffle of a kitten's fur.

The Chinese *A. japonica*, syn. *A. hupehensis*, flowering in mid-autumn—some three to four feet high—also produces some beautiful leaves, as does the small *A. blanda*, and *A. nemorosa* (the lovely Wood Anemone or wild Windflower).

It is important that all anemone leaves be pressed lying flat, as otherwise they may curl. They should have several weeks' pressing before use.

Presumably the somewhat sad little anemone face earned its Language of Flowers meaning: forsaken.

AQUILEGIA——*Ranunculaceæ*——COLUMBINE

Flowers of that respect, as that no Garden would willingly be without them.

John Parkinson: *Paradisus*

The early summer garden forms produce some exquisite seed-heads, invaluable for dried arrangements.

The Columbine genus is vast in number, covering a large part of the world. Of the two wild forms, *A. vulgaris* grows on shady slopes and in woods, mainly on chalk, and *A. pyrenaica* is now a native in the Caenlochan Glen among the Clova Mountains of Angus. All are worth the collector's attention.

A watch needs to be kept on the seed-heads once they are formed, although they should not be picked until they open in their outward-curving shapes.

In his *Flowers in History*, Peter Coats refers to Memling's painting, dated 1490, which shows a majolica vase full of lilies, iris and columbines—the latter, with their dove-shaped flowers, symbolising the Holy Ghost.

ARBUTUS——*A. Unedo*——*Ericaceæ*——THE KILLARNEY STRAWBERRY TREE

It delyteth some men for the diversyte.

William Turner: *Herball*

It is tender and never comes to any considerable bignes with us.

Sir Thomas Hanmer

An ornamental garden shrub or small tree of great distinction with outstanding reddened stems, to be found in southern Europe and growing wild in Ireland, and much valued in sheltered positions in discriminating gardens. Its end-tapering toothed leaves are of lustrous green quality, perfect to look at, and perfect too for the collector to preserve. They press easily and retain their beautiful colour. Other species might be well worth attention, although no experiments have yet been carried out.

ASPERULA——*Rubiaceæ*——WOODRUFF

They that write of this herbe give it greate commendation for making of the herte merry.

William Turner: *Herball*

Though there is nothing to equal *Galium verum* (Lady's Bedstraw), which is described on page 119, no list would be complete without mention of its cousin, the square-stemmed *Asperula* (Woodruff), growing from Europe to North Africa, in Asia and in Australia.

The silvery leaves of the early summer-flowering rock garden *A. suberosa* from Greece dry well after the pretty lilac-pink flowers have been removed. *A. odorata*, syn. *Galium odorata* (Sweet Woodruff) is a sweet-scented species with white flowers. It was cultivated in gardens in Turner's time, at the beginning of Elizabeth's reign—"The floures," he remarked, "are whyte and well-smellinge"—and frequently dried for its fragrance. Why not continue this custom—and dry enough for arrangements at the same time? Dry the stems, leaves and flowers *in their entirety*, by gentle pressing, and trim as required when assembling.

A. cynanchica (Squinancy-wort) is a somewhat branching, prostrate plant with dainty leaves, which gets its vernacular name from its reputation as a cure for the quinsy.

ASTRANTIA——*Umbelliferæ*——MASTERWORT, HATTIE'S PINCUSHION

A. maxima is the most widely grown garden form of these herbaceous perennials from the East Caucasus, and when picked in full summer bloom, and dried slowly and naturally, it makes a most charmingly delicate addition to any arrangement.

Its group of flower-heads—some wide and others half-open—has a stem strong enough not to need wiring. Hence it should be picked reasonably full-length, stripped of leaves and stored standing up in a pot or carton.

Astrantia is a small genus, but it has a long history. Its name, charmingly and appropriately, means "star-like". William Hanbury, the eighteenth century cleric and scholar whose collections of plants were valued at £10,000, disliked it and saw no real beauty in its flowers. "The very worst part of the garden should be assigned to them." How horrid and wrong he was. Gerard, on the other hand, valued it highly, though for its "vertue" rather than its beauty: "Not only good against all poison, but singular against all corrupt and naughtie aire and infection of the pestilence."

Be this as it may, a collection of astrantia flowers is all-important to the discriminating collector, and greatly helps to enhance any dried arrangement.

AUCUBA——*Cornaceæ*

These shining evergreen shrubs, some of which are natives of Asia, Japan and the Himalayas, are splendid settlers in sheltered positions in the shrub border or the cool green-house. The species most commonly grown is *A. japonica* (Spotted Laurel). Its leaves are pale yellow spotted with dark green, or vice versa. The variegated form—*A. j. maculata*—is aptly termed Gold Dust Tree. Though, alas, the lovely red berries do not preserve well, the leaves can be successfully pressed or glycerined, and form most useful material for the base of a dried arrangement.

BALLOTA——*Labiatæ*

B. Pseudodictamnus comes from Crete, and is a most decorative plant, both in the garden border and in dried arrangements.

Like delphiniums and *Alchemilla Mollis*, ballota poses a query: whether to gather it whilst it is still young and green (as should be done for perfect preserving) or leave it to play its part—undoubtedly an attractive one—in the garden landscape. The gardener and dried collector should come to terms in their best interests respectively! If left for harvesting until late autumn, ballota will even then be useful, but it will have taken on a silvery-fawn hue and may appear somewhat mournful. When gathering, do not divest it of the heart-shaped, fluffy leaves. Hang it upside down or lay it flat to dry. When ready for assembling, decide which leaves can be retained. The earlier it is picked, the better the leaves will preserve and the whiter the stems will remain.

Though a small genus, ballota has many august kinsmen—for instance, the balm *Melissa officinalis*, so beloved of bees, the beautiful fragrant bergamot, the ground ivy or gill-on-the-ground, the field balm and the canary balm—all with histories told and retold by herbalists of bygone days.

BERGENIA, syn. MEGASEA——*Saxifragaceæ*

This most lovable of pathside plants, a favourite with Gertrude Jekyll, is aptly described as Elephant's Ear Saxifrage or Pig-squeak. A garden without some of the species of this ideal evergreen ground-cover, adding leaf contrast at the edge of a border or filling a gap, would be noticeably incomplete.

The large leaves should have the glycerine treatment (page 63), and the smaller ones can be pressed. Although no experience is yet to hand, there should be little reason why the flowers might not be preserved in silica gel (page 61). Before attempting to preserve any of the leaves, gently wash or spray them, as being ground-hugging they are liable to get spattered with soil during seasonal forking-over of the surrounding earth.

B. cordifolia and *B. purpurea* from Siberia are the most commonly grown, and provide throughout the year an exciting sequence of different coloured foliage. The violet-pink flowers of *B. Delavayi*, from the Yunnan, are very decorative.

BUXUS——*B. sempervirens*——*Buxaceæ*——COMMON BOX

This accommodating evergreen tree, so well adapted from Roman times to verdant architecture and topiary, has sombre funereal associations, and its subtle qualities may not, at first, inspire the collector.

It can be found growing happily as a small tree over much of the world, in Great Britain flourishing wild—particularly on Box Hill in Surrey, and on the Chilterns, Cotswolds, Downs and in other chalky districts—and it should not be ignored. If allowed to pursue its own course it grows gracefully, with tough little leathery leaves, dark on the upper side and attractively pale green beneath. These features may not especially excite the fresh flower arranger, but this invaluable shrub is, without exception, one of the mainstays of the dried collector's leaf-and-spray store. The trouble is in finding a free-growing natural specimen, with its pretty four-angled winged branches, rather than a tree which has been the victim of garden shears used for ornamental topiary work. From early ages box has endured torment in the interests of what was, admittedly, great beauty.

Sprays of box leaves should be dried in quantity, by pressing very lightly, anywhere and everywhere—even, as an exception (low be it spoken), under the carpet! It also responds well to glycerine treatment (page 63). Whatever drying method is used, no store can be complete without this shrub. It forms a perfect base for all dried arrangements, and helps to cover Plasticine foundation settings. There are several forms of *B. sempervirens*—some attractively yellow-tinted and variegated.

All down the ages men have adorned their gardens with clipped box edgings and fantastic growths of box trimmed into the shapes of heraldic beasts, legendary creatures, nymphs and birds and labyrinths; they have even had their own names clipped out in evergreen box. Decorative topiary work apart, box has many uses, several of which derive from the extreme heaviness of the wood, which is dense and even in grain. Turner disposed briskly of its herbal value: "The wood of Boxe is yellowe and pale and serveth for no use in medicine that I have red of."

CAMELLIA——*Theaceæ*

Camellia flowers have no scent but their blooms, and indeed their foliage, have an unrivalled beauty of form. They are of immensely ancient lineage. Joseph Kamel, a Moravian-born Jesuit priest, and a botanist of great merit and reputation, will forever be associated with the distribution of their seeds from eastern gardens, for the genus was named after him, in his honour.

The attention of the dried flower arranger should be directed to the matchless importance of the beautifully shining evergreen foliage, which lasts in water, and which can be preserved in glycerine, or pressed. The double blooms retain their superb colour and elegance miraculously well if preserved in silica gel. For information on the varieties of the *C. japonica* species, a study of specialist nurserymen's lists is advised.

No story of this most exquisite of all earthly flowers would be complete without reference to the two "camellia" heroines: Marguerite of *La Dame aux Camelias*, and Violetta of *La Traviata*. Marguerite always wore the beautiful scentless camellias because perfume made her cough.

In the Language of Flowers the white camellia denotes unpretending excellence, whilst its red-flowered counterpart expresses rare loveliness.

CENTAUREA——*Compositæ*——KNAPWEED, BLUE-BOTTLE
Good against the inflammation of the eies.

John Gerard: *Herball*

The garden perennial from the Caucasus, *C. dealbata*, will produce quite exquisite dried seed-heads which resemble silvery-fawn flowers (they appear in Fig. 26 on page 77).

The garden plant needs to be watched as soon as it starts flowering, from midsummer to early autumn, and as each seed-head opens it should be gathered separately, in order to keep it dry. Earlier in the season, some of the unopened buds can be gathered and varnished. Centaurea seed-heads need no special treatment for drying—just careful storing, loosely upright. *C. dealbata*

"John Coutts" can also provide good seed-heads. The unopened buds of many of the wild knapweeds and cornflowers can be varnished and dried, laid flat on paper, in the same way as clematis seed-heads (this process is described on page 66).

CHOISYA——*C. ternata*——*Rutaceæ*——MEXICAN ORANGE

This native of Mexico and member of the rue family has graced selected sheltered corners in English gardens since the mid-nineteenth century. Named after a Swiss cleric and botanist, it is an outstandingly impressive evergreen shrub, some ten feet high. Its glossy, digitately-compound, green aromatic leaves are rightly prized by flower arrangers—both for fresh and dried use. They preserve very happily, either by pressing (page 60), or in glycerine (page 63). Like osmanthus—now called siphonosmanthus—they should be cut as sprays, so long as the mound-like form of the shrub is not impaired. Leaves that have caught the sun's rays will be yellower than those facing the shade. Both are attractive, but only mature leaves should be harvested. The fragrant waxy white Mexican orange-blossom is also good for preserving in silica gel—and according to William Robinson, a spray of choisya cut in autumn will remain fresh until the following spring.

CLARKIA——*Onagraceæ*

This genus is a small one. Two of its species, *C. pulchella* from Oregon and *C. elegans* from California, are the parents of those charming hardy annuals listed in seed catalogues, which no summer garden (or indeed, dried flower arranger) should be without. They have fascinating crinkly flowers, often double, grown in clusters, in raceme form. Delightful too are their cousins, "Fairy Fans" and "Red Ribbons".

A goodly quantity of seed of the different varieties should be sown each spring, as demands on the plants will be heavy and three-fold—first for garden colour, and for fresh flower arranging in quantity; and for the dried seed-head collector. Clarkia can also be grown in pots in the green-house. They dry easily on their own stems, either upside down, or laid flat, and make a very effective addition to the store. They last well, and retain their colour.

Sprays of these charming flowers are said to mean, "Will you dance with me?"

CLEMATIS——*Ranunculaceæ*——VIRGIN'S BOWER

This enormous genus, especially in its staggeringly beautiful climbing garden forms, provides the arranger with a wealth of fascinating seed-heads. Among the large-flowered varieties, "Nelly Moser", "Barbara Dibley", "Mrs Cholmondeley" and others are quite invaluable. So also are the spring-flowering *C. macropetala* and *C. alpina* varieties, and the very late-flowering *C. Jouiniana*—the latter with its white fluffy inflorescence makes a most ethereal addition to any arrangement, and is a beautiful feature of Fig. 19 on page 65.

All these seed-heads require attention immediately they are picked. They can either be processed dry and hairy, or varnished shiny and stiff—a mixture of both forms in an arrangement lends great interest (as in Fig. 7 on page 37, for example). In the first case, the head is allowed to become fluffy before it is picked—then twirled in a circular movement in the fingers to collect the "back hair" and gently sprayed *at the back only* with a light hair lacquer to fix. In the second case, the head is immersed in transparent varnish immediately after picking—no waiting till next day—and then laid on several thicknesses of newspaper to drain. The newspaper should be replaced with fresh sheets at intervals of a few hours thereafter, until the heads are completely stiff and dry and ready for storing in flat open boxes to await arrangement.

C. Jouiniana, the very late-flowering hybrid, needs no special treatment other than drying loosely upright. It should be picked with fairly long stems just as it starts to become fluffy, as this process will continue more satisfactorily under cover of protection from a damp atmosphere.

Clematis leaves in their delicate shapes are well worth collecting and pressing gently, and when dry will last for many months. They are excellent for drooping at the front of an arrangement.

CROCOSMIA——*Iridaceæ*

Tritonia crocosmæflora (Montbretia) is one of a large and variable group of late-flowering corms. Another is *Curtonus paniculatus*, syn. *Antholyza paniculata*, with its equally beautiful, montbretia-like, flame-coloured flower-heads. All are excellent for harvesting for dried arrangements. The arching sprays of seed-heads should be gathered almost before the last petals have dropped. They can be dried flat, or better still, varnished, and they make extremely attractive outlining material, quite indispensable for dried work. Some of the smaller long leaves are useful for pressing, and are very long-lasting.

CYTISUS——*Leguminosæ*——BROOM

> *The decoction of twigs and tops of broom doth cleanse and open the liver, milt and kidnies.*
>
> John Gerard: *Herball*

The species of the *Cytisus*, *Genista* and *Spartium* genera are much alike except for small botanical differences, and consequently botanists have shifted them backwards and forwards from one to another. Their main interest for the flower arranger lies in the graceful bending sprays which can be carefully coaxed into slender arching shapes to give the required line to an arrangement.

For drying, choose only the more delicate sprays from the tips of the shrubs. These can be damped, shaped into curves, lightly tied with silk or thin strips of sellotape, and dried between sheets of blotting paper. Among the many nurserymen's varieties, *C. præcox* (Warminster Broom) is good, as indeed are other small young forms. These are frequently used as temporary gap-fillers in garden design, and are in consequence very adaptable to the dried collector's needs. The shining silvery foliage of *C. Battandieri* also presses or preserves well. The native British *C. scoparius*, syn. *Spartium scoparium* (Scottish Broom), so widely distributed on heathland throughout the country, needs no description; only the young sprays should be collected, as they adapt better for dried work.

DELPHINIUM——*Ranunculaceæ*

The annual larkspur, *D. Ajacis*, and its double forms in white, pink, mauve and blue, are of infinite importance to the dried flower collector, and no effort should be spared to grow them in large quantities for cutting and preserving. They can also be bought from florists, and in markets.

Our magnificent garden delphiniums descend from the larkspurs Gerard knew. He believed that the seed and leaf were useful in fending off "any venemous beast". The name larkspur—*pied d'alouette*—is contracted from one of the old names he lists—"larkes-spurs, larkes-heels, larkes-toes, larkes-claws". John Parkinson knew them too: "Larks heeles, or spurres, or toes, as in severall countries they are called, exceed in the varietie of colours, both single and double, any of the former times . . . the single Kindes are reasonable well disperst over the Land, yet the double Kindes of all these pleasant colours . . . which stand like little double Roses, are enjoyed but of a few." He treated them as annuals, but thereafter the great delphinium breeders—James Kelway, Amos Perry and others—began to cultivate the magnificent perennial hybrids found in our herbaceous borders today.

The delphinium is reputed to have been christened by Dioscorides, its name deriving from the Greek word for the dolphin—the unopened buds being said to resemble dolphins ("A certain shew and likenesse," according to Gerard): an idea seemingly far-fetched, but quite realistic if a group of young plants is seen against the sunlight—though even then, as Alice Coats remarks in *Flowers and their Histories*, the resemblance is nearer to that of a tadpole!

The larger-flowering delphinium hybrids, such as *D. Belladonna*, provide not only superb colours to preserve but also, later on, seed-heads to dry—this conflict of interests can only be resolved by great diplomacy and ingenuity when harvesting! Good specimens of leaves can be pressed. Flower-heads can be tied together and dried hanging upside down, preferably in a hot airing cupboard (as described on page 60). Watch them daily, and when the petals sound crisp to the touch, remove them to the store. The seed-heads should be dried flat. When gathering flower-heads, make certain to include some unopened buds on the terminal and lateral spikes, to add lightness and delicacy in arrangements. There are some fine spires of larkspur in the arrangement illustrated on page 45.

In the Language of Flowers the blue larkspur suggests fickleness; the purple variety, haughtiness.

DIGITALIS——*Scrophulariaceæ*——FOXGLOVE
A large genus—native from Europe to Central Asia, and growing wild and cultivated in Britain.

Seed-heads of both sorts are of use in drying, and there is much choice in height and size. The seedsmen's catalogues list several magnificent hardy perennial and biennial hybrids, and all are excellent for the dried flower collector, except, perhaps, *D. Mertonensis*, the seed-heads of which are somewhat out of scale. The "Excelsior" hybrids of *D. purpurea* are well worth cultivating, not only for the exquisite art shades of their flowers, but also for their graceful racemes which when dry are quite invaluable for arrangements. It is the topmost and upper portions of the flower-spray which should be used, put on a wire stalk for easier working. The wild form of *D. purpurea*, so often seen in woodland clearings and on heaths, is of great value to the dried flower collector because of its smaller scale.

The foxglove features frequently in ancient herbals, and the drug digitalis is still much in use for diseases of the heart. Foxgloves have had many names, often sombre ones—Precious Bane, for instance, which Mary Webb used for the title of her novel. The generic name comes from the Latin *digis*, "a finger"—thus, finger-flower. Some botanists suggest that "glove" is a corruption of the Anglo Saxon *gliew*—"music", and that foxgloves are accordingly named after an ancient musical instrument—a ring of bells on an arched support. Alice Coats gives the best old-fashioned name of all: the simple, cheerful "floppy-dock".

In the Language of Flowers this bloom is said to indicate insincerity.

ECHINOPS——*Compositæ*——GLOBE THISTLE
The Greek name means "hedgehog-like"—and how true! *E. Ritro* is to be found growing in most summer herbaceous borders, and is a native of East Europe and West Asia. Its steel-blue spherical heads are prickly-looking, and shaped like drumsticks. A careful watch should be kept to ensure picking well before the pale blue flowers are out. Harvesting should preferably be on a dry day. They dry best hung upside down. In assembling, the arranger may find the prickly heads easier to handle if they are put on false wire stems extending about halfway up their natural stems. The silver-backed, much-divided foliage is also useful, and can be pressed.

Mr E. A. Bowles said of echinops: "I have often recommended them for entomologists' gardens, where plants are grown so that they can be visited after dark with a lantern to surprise a supper party of noctuid moths!"

The species of echinops are numerous—growing in an area reaching from Portugal and Spain to India and central Asia, and covering Africa as well—and no doubt many of them would be useful to the dried flower collector.

ELÆAGNUS——*Elæagnaceæ*——OLEASTER

These mostly evergreen and ornamental shrubs, akin to sea-buckthorn, are very pleasing in shrub borders, and it is a pity that more of them are not seen. They are so different from each other, but all give an impression of growing in an atmosphere of haze, except in the evening when the failing light seems to catch the silvery, sometimes variegated, glow on their leaves and relieve their daytime air of melancholy.

First and foremost one must mention *E. ebbingei* (a hybrid of *E. macrophylla* and *E. pungens*) and doubly underline its importance for the dried leaf collector. These olive-green leaves with their silver-white or oyster backs should, if possible, be gathered in hundreds during the course of the year. They press and dry extremely well and easily, and should, together with rhododendron and laurel leaves, create the base of all stores. Their slightly bent leaf-stalks should be given false wires (page 84), unless a terminal spray is used. These leaves will last for many years between sheets of blotting paper and still retain their suppleness and intriguing colour. The variegated leaves of *E. pungens aureo-variegata*—*E. p. aureo-maculata*—and *E. p. Dicksonii*, too, are of great beauty and should be collected wherever possible.

Elæagnus species are to be found in Europe, West Asia, North America, China and Japan.

ENDYMION——*E. Hispanica,* syn. *Scilla campanulata*——*Liliaceæ*——SPANISH BLUEBELL

These bulbs like large bluebells, are listed in bulb catalogues in series of fantastically beautiful colours. They are named after an exotic youth in Greek mythology who was loved by Selene, goddess of the moon. She bore him fifty daughters, and then, finding his passion and its consequences too tiring, caused him to fall into everlasting sleep so that she could simply kiss him gently as much as she pleased. Lying there in his perpetual sleep, he has never grown a day older, but still looks young and beautiful.

Be this as it may, this scilla should not be harvested until the spikes of lovely seed-heads have dried and are crisp to the touch, which will depend on the weather. When once picked, they can be stored upright or flat. They form the basis of some of the most ethereal arrangements, and are quite essential for dried flower work. They require careful handling. Should the hollow stems become brittle, they can be strengthened by inserting stub wire. They can then be gently bent into curves for assembly.

The English native bluebell—*Scilla nutans,* syn. *S. nonscripta*—lovely as it is for naturalising, is not a successful subject for drying.

116

EPILOBIUM——*E. angustifolium,* syn. *Chamænerion angustifolium*——*Onagraceæ*——ROSE
BAY WILLOW-HERB, FIREWEED

This most beautiful of the willow-herbs—growing in large pink and grey drifts in sunny parts of woodland clearings, and frequently too found in quarries and on demolished building sites and burnt waste ground—should be gathered the very moment the petals fall and as soon as the seed-heads begin to curl—and how indeed they try to curl—right up the tapering pink stalk from the lower leaves to the topmost point.

Rose bay willow-herb can be preserved in two ways:

1. by leaving it to dry naturally and allowing its curling seed-heads to become fluffy and hairy; or
2. far more attractively, by varnishing immediately after picking and laying flat on paper to dry.

The two methods are exactly similar to those advised on page 113 for preserving clematis heads. The dried willow-herb should be stored standing upright. No doubt the same preserving techniques could be carried out with good effect with other members of the *Epilobium* genus—but *E. angustifolium* (Rose Bay) has a more impressive inflorescence and is very easy to come by.

EPIMEDIUM——*Berberidaceæ*——BARRENWORT, BISHOP'S HAT

Once more the gardener's search for labour-saving ground-cover will be of help—in this instance, intriguing help—to the collector—but on one condition: the tender leaves may not be picked until the plants have finished flowering (in early spring) or frost may attack the unprotected flowers, which are delicate and quite beautiful. No matter—the later the entrancing leaves are picked, having been left to don their late summer hues, the better—and all should then go smoothly! Miss Jekyll described them as delightful at every season—for many of them are evergreen; the tints of the spring leaves, which follow the flowers, are charming; and in the autumn, as she says, they "fall into tone with the season with such rich shades of russet, brown and gold". Indeed, these pinnate, pointed, heart-shaped leaves, which look fragile but are in reality quite tough, and which grow on very long stems, provide indispensable leaf material, whether fresh or dried, for the flower arranger, and are of especial merit for the base of an arrangement.

To dry these leaves can be tricky because of the peculiar way their stems are tucked back and beneath them. They should be pressed in the way they grow; later, during assembly, wire can be added to the stem to achieve, if necessary, an easier line.

The *Epimedium* genus has a number of species, all full of charm, and many evergreen or nearly so. Perhaps the loveliest form, from Japan and Manchuria, is *E. grandiflorum* "Rose Queen"—though *E. versicolor sulphureum*, with its marbled leaves, is just as enchanting; and nurserymen's catalogues list many more.

ERYNGIUM——*Umbelliferæ*

A large genus of over two hundred species, mostly perennials—but also some seaside plants—*E. maritimum* (Sea Holly), for instance—growing wild. *E. tripartitum*, with its very blue thistle, is a charmer, as also is *E. giganteum*, from the Caucasus.

Being very spiky, they are difficult to handle, and inserting wire into the centre of the hollow stems may make the task of the arranger easier. In many species the glistening, metallic, bluish sheen of the stem—and the inflorescence of the floral bract—are features of supreme beauty. All dry easily hung upside down, and they add attraction to a dried arrangement.

The *Eryngium* genus is of ancient lineage and it features in herbals from mediaeval times.

FRITILLARIA——*Liliaceæ*——FRITILLARY

> *I know what white, what purple fritillaries,*
> *The grassy harvest of the river-fields,*
> *Above by Ensham, down by Sandford, yields—*
>
> Matthew Arnold: *Thyrsis*

A very ancient and quite enchanting genus; each one is full of individuality and charm, though the roots of some have a peculiar nauseous smell. They are mostly hardy and are to be found growing in both hemispheres.

F. meleagris (the Snake's Head or Guinea-fowl Flower) which grows wild in Britain, is also to be found from the Scandinavian peninsula to the Balkans. John Gerard knew it well: "Some calling it Flos Meleagridis, the Ginny Hen Flower, of the variety of the colours in the flower, agreeing with the feathers of that Bird. Some call it N. [Narcissus] Caparonius, of the name of the first inventor or finder thereof"—Capron, its French discoverer, was murdered in the Massacre of St Bartholomew's Eve. "It is now generally called Fritillaria, of the word Fritillus, which divers doe take for the Chesse borde or table whereon they play, whereunto, by reason of the resemblance of the great squares or spots so like it, they did presently referre it." *F. meleagris* has several superb varieties, all invaluable to the seed-head collector. John Parkinson spoke, so rightly, of "the gallant beauty of many of them", and it seems hard that this exquisite and best-known chequered lily with its purple and maroon tinted and spotted bells should have found disfavour with Miss Sackville West, who called it

> *Sullen and foreign looking, the snakey flower*
> *Scarfed in dull purple.*

Poor little gem—in all its small height of some twelve to fifteen inches, it has had to put up with many unkind names. In *Flowers and their Histories*, Alice Coats lists Sullen Lady, Drooping Tulip, Turkey Eggs, Madame Ugly, Widow's Veil, Toad's Heads; and there are others too unkind to mention. It is rather what someone has called "a snatch of grace beyond the reach of art".

Notwithstanding its nicknames, the collector of seed-heads should spare no pains to ensure a source of supply. A possible source is a private garden originally stocked by bulb and seed nurserymen. The harvester must keep a careful watch in early summer, for while in flower the fritillary hangs its head daintily, but when the seeds ripen the stems turn upwards and the small seed-capsules look upwards to the sky. When picking, collect the seeds for sowing and dry the seed-heads and their slender stems gently, on the flat. They can be varnished if desired.

Finally, the Language of Flowers rightly names the fritillary persecution, probably because of the legend that its majestic cousin, the crown imperial, was the only flower which did not bow its head as Our Lord passed by to Calvary—and has for ever after hung it weeping in shame.

GALIUM——*Rubiaceæ*——BEDSTRAW

A family of slender summer-flowering herbs, mostly with square stems—some growing upright, some trailing, others matted, procumbent or scrambling—with small, narrow, slightly shiny leaves and a riot of tiny delicate yellow or white flowers growing in panicles.

Though it is sometimes cultivated in rock gardens, or its cut flowers included in a florist's bouquet to give a filmy effect, it is seen at its best and most fairy-like when growing wild. (The white *G. Mollugo*—"False Baby's Breath"—is often confused with *Gypsophila paniculata*, but it is, in fact, entirely different.) The collector should turn to the hedgerow and the outer edges of fields and banks, sunny or shady and damp. It sometimes grows on peat, sometimes in chalky places. The greatest gem, often come by in dry places, is the native British *G. verum* (Lady's Bedstraw) which can also be found growing in Europe, Russian Asia, and North America.

It should be ready to pick in July and August, and September, but care must be taken to harvest just as the flowers are before, or at, their best. Harvest them on a dry day—it is no use gathering them when they are wet or blackened by loss of colour. The stem, leaves and flowers should be lightly pressed, being placed *in their entirety* between sheets of blotting paper and given under-a-sofa-cushion treatment. The result will be a collection of light, transparent, diaphanous sprigs essential for outlining arrangements. They should be among the "top ten" in any worker's pickings.

For equally alluring family traits, reference should be made to the more sophisticated member of this stellate tribe—*Asperula* (Woodruff) which is described on page 108.

GALTONIA——*G. candicans*——*Liliaceæ*——GIANT SUMMER HYACINTH

This late-flowering South African bulb, also known as *Hyacinthus candicans*, is a tall and stately white-flowered subject for the herbaceous border or the outer edges of a shrub garden. No garden should be without it, and no dried material collector should rest until a supply of the magnificent candelabra-shaped scapes of seed-heads can be acquired. They should be harvested as soon as, or even before, the last petals have fallen, unless the late summer is particularly hot when they will dry on their own. The hollow stems will take a long time to dry, and they may do best when cut and hung upside down.

Gerard maintained that its hyacinth cousins would "bring the haire again in places which have been burned or scalded".

GERANIUM——*Geraniaceæ*——CRANESBILL

Cureth miraculously ruptures or burstings, as myselfe hath often prooved, whereby I have gotten crownes and credite.

John Gerard: *Herball*

A large genus of quite enchanting plants, both cultivated and wild. Most of the cultivated cranesbills, with the exception of pelargoniums, are natives of Britain or very early introductions from Europe.

From the dried arranger's point of view, it is the palmately lobed or deeply divided leaves which are of such importance; this applies alike to the herbaceous garden, rock garden, and wild pasture species, but does not normally include the florists' type of pelargonium. The cranesbills, as a race, are beautiful, hardy, and amenable to cultivation; grown in sun or shade, they are clump-making, thus providing splendid ground-cover—a fact which gives the collector plenty of opportunity for choosing good shapely specimens for drying. In his writings Mr A. T. Johnson says that he is astonished to find how infrequently hardy geraniums feature in the ordinary garden. "They fit into their surroundings with the subtle sympathy which weds harebell to heath". And how right he is—a challenge to the arranger to grow his own, or to seek out in other gardens a supply from which he can pick.

The daintily cut foliage—some with attractive autumn colour—dries easily between sheets of blotting paper and is very long-lasting; this applies equally to cultivated and wild forms. To a lesser degree, some of the delicate seed-heads can be harvested if in good condition. Admittedly hard to find and tricky to preserve, they are well worth the effort in spite of their fragility. Of the cultivated species, *G. Endressii* from the Pyrenees has elegant light green leaves. *G. Endressii* "Wargrave", with its dense tufts of attractive leaves, is worth searching for. *G. ibericum* var. *G. platypetalum*, from the Caucasus, has beautiful autumn-coloured foliage worth harvesting. Among the cultivated species with good leaves are *G. ibericum* "Johnson's Blue"; *G. sanguineum* (the Bloody Cranesbill) from Europe and Western Asia, with its hummock of deeply lobed filigree leaves; *G. pratense* (the native British Meadow Cranesbill, which is also known as the Crowfoot Cranesbill); and *G. sylvaticum* (Wood Cranesbill). Failing cultivated forms, the collector would do well to look for the equally captivating wild varieties growing in meadows, on banksides, on cliffs—in shade as well as in sunshine. These leaves and seed-heads could be invaluable. The whole cranesbill tribe can, indeed, furnish the dried leaf store with a commodity *par excellence*—and some beautiful seed-heads as well.

The Language of Flowers mentions various meanings, such as melancholy, bridal favour, an expected meeting, true friendship, preference, comforting, and steadfast piety.

GODETIA——*Onagraceæ*

The many varieties of this Californian hardy garden annual form most attractive clustered seed-heads, useful for drying. They should be harvested in late summer when the colourful flower display is over. The tall or medium varieties are the best for drying. The stems dry well, but the leaves should be stripped off. Dry flat. Any of the seedsmen's varieties will do well.

GOMPHRENA —— *G. globosa* —— *Amaranthaceæ* —— GLOBE AMARANTH, SPANISH CLOVER

> *Bid Amaranthus all his beauty shed.*
>
> John Milton: *Lycidas*

This charming little immortelle—so greatly loved in Victorian times—has come back on the market as Spanish Clover. It is a half-hardy annual, emanating mainly from South America and India, and it is best if grown under cover, to protect the flowers. Any of the seedsmen's varieties are useful for preserving, and should be harvested as soon as the flower-heads are fully grown.

HEDERA——*Araliaceæ*——IVY

> *Five of the berries beaten small and made hot in a Pomegranate rinde with oile of Roses, and dropped into the contrarie Eare, doth ease the toothache . . . The cluster berries make the haire blacke.*
>
> John Gerard, reporting the opinion of Dioscorides: *Herball*

These evergreen shrubs, climbing by rootlets, are very varied and ornamental in foliage and growth. As Alice Coats so rightly says in *Garden Shrubs and their Histories*, "Ivy harbours as many legends and traditions as it does spiders, and its literature, like the plant itself, must be severely pruned to keep it within reasonable bounds." The Greeks and the Romans both valued it: the plant was sacred to Dionysus (Bacchus), the god of wine; his maenad followers drank a highly intoxicating drink laced with ivy and celebrated the mysteries of his cult in an adoring frenzy. Among the god's attributes were his ivy-wreathed thyrsus and his ivy chaplet. Hence the use of ivy as a tavern sign—an English alehouse keeper would simply nail a bundle of ivy over his door—and hence too the mediaeval proverb "Good wine needs no bush". The great mediaeval hall was hung with ivy at Christmastide; its eternal green made it a symbol of life enduring and surviving the rigours of winter.

The variety of enchanting forms makes it indispensable to the gardener, whether it be for climbing over walls or as ground-cover, or for hanging from urns on the patio, or to drape a window-box; and it is equally valuable to the fresh or dried flower arranger. Leaves of every shape and diversity, particularly those which are heart-shaped at the base, are essential for the latter's store—they press easily, take up glycerine well, and can, when mature, be varnished, although the green leaves retain their natural colour better than the beautiful variegated ones. *H. Helix* (the common English ivy) and many of its cultivars, will be found invaluable—and a search in a green-house, conservatory, or through the lists of the nurserymen will be well worth-while to secure the others. (Trails of variegated ivy were used in the arrangement of fresh and dried material on page 65.) In dried material arranging, if some of the ivy leaves are tough or show signs of being intractable, fine wire, fixed along the back of the mid-vein with sellotape, and then wound round the leaf stalk, will help greatly in manipulating.

Gerard, listing its "vertues", declared that ivy was "very seldome used" in his England. He did, however, recommend it for sores, for kidney trouble, and for smarting eyes, so it had evidently not fallen into complete oblivion. Alice Coats quotes an Andrew Marvell reference, half a century later: "There is nothing more natural than for it to be of the opinion that the oak cannot stand without its support." It draped the ruins and grottoes of the late eighteenth century—"As creeping ivy clings to wood or stone," wrote Cowper, with settled gloom, "And hides the ruin that it feeds upon"; and was echoed by Bailey, "For ivy climbs the crumbling hall to decorate decay." Its fortunes have twined like the plant itself, and in view of the way some of its past history dips into melancholy and gloom, it is good to note its present-day happy and colourful existence in fresh and fascinating forms, and its unquestionable usefulness to the flower arranger.

In the Language of Flowers ivy stands for friendship, fidelity, and marriage, and a sprig of the plant means assiduity to please.

HERACLEUM——*Umbelliferæ*——COW PARSNIP

For the vast number of the cartwheel types of this umbellifer, one generally turns to wild vegetation, unless one can find some growing in an aromatic herb garden. This includes parsley, chervil, fennel, cow parsley, angelica, and their kindred tribes. The flat umbels of the differing forms and sizes can be very beautiful in a dried arrangement, especially seen against the light.

Picking this multitudinous number of varieties is not particularly easy, as the heads are so fragile and nearly always at varying stages of ripeness all on one plant. Harvesting must, therefore, be done at more than one time—just as the seed-heads are formed, and again before bad weather sets in and takes its toll. Once gathered, the fragile heads should be dried loosely upright, and if possible some may be gently varnished. Angelica heads can be pulled apart, and each floret used singly when dried and wired. The leaves, too, can be pressed.

For a detailed study of this prolific tribe of umbelliferae, Mr Keble Martin's *The Concise British Flora* will be more than helpful.

HYDRANGEA——*Saxifragaceæ*

These ornamental woody plants, mostly deciduous shrubs, are justly prized by flower arrangers throughout the world. Though most of the leaves press well and are well worth collecting, it is the large round snowball-like flower-heads, full of coloured bracts, which are invaluable to the fresh and dried flower worker alike—but chiefly to the latter. They feature in several of the arrangements shown in the book; Fig. 26 on page 77 is just one example.

The name "hydrangea" is derived from the Greek words for "water" and "vessel", referring to the shape of its fruits—some of which are attractive to dry. It is a large genus, many species coming from China, Japan and the United States. The common *H. macrophylla* is divided into two groups—Lacecaps and Hortensias; and it is the latter type, with rounded heads of sterile florets or bracts, which are of use in drying. So too are the heads of the tree-like *H. paniculata*, and above all the smaller, and far more delicate, globular cream-coloured heads of *H. cinerea sterilis*. This is a real "must" for the dried material collector's store.

The important and sometimes tricky process of gathering and drying hydrangea heads is discussed in detail on pages 52–53, and their wiring is shown in Fig. 15 on page 53.

No garden could be considered complete without the inclusion of some hydrangeas; nor could the store of the dried material collector, who should keep an ample quantity in reserve.

IBERIS——*Cruciferæ*——CANDYTUFT

Gather in somer good plentye of this roote for then it hath most vertue and bete it harde . . . and mix it wyth swines gresse . . . then if any man or woman have any paine in the haunch or huckel bone binde this oyntment upon the place.

William Turner: *Herball*

In the Language of Flowers this most sprightly and friendly-faced crucifer represents indifference —very unfairly, it would seem. Only the garden-cultivated types are of use in dried arranging, but *how* useful! Their gay and fascinating seed-heads lend lightness and delicacy, and will last for years. Their stems, too, dry well, so do not require wires. It is as well not to strip all the leaves off before drying, as some retain their natural shapes and after suitable varnishing can enhance the whole.

Both the species for garden decoration are hardy annuals, and are listed in many different shades in seed catalogues. *I. coronaria hyacinthiflora* is the Rocket or Giant-flowered Candytuft, with fragrant flowers growing in spiral racemes which elongate with age. The dried heads are impressively graceful and should always be harvested soon after flowering is over. *I. umbellata* (the common garden Candytuft) in all its rainbow colours is even more valuable for dried arranging, but the exact time for harvesting depends on when the seed-heads are widely open, which in turn depends on sunny weather. It is a good idea to dip the gathered umbels immediately in varnish and to dry them flat on newspaper (see page 66), which should be changed frequently to prevent their sticking to it. The final result should prove one of the most successful and indispensable treasures—to be stored upright in quantity.

IRIS——Iridaceæ

> *Good for them that suffer from cramps and convulsions and for such as are bit with serpents.*
>
> John Gerard: *Herball*

> *. . . Heaven is free*
> *From clouds, but of all colours seems to be—*
> *Melted to one vast Iris of the West—*
> *Where the Day joins the past Eternity.*
>
> Lord Byron: *Childe Harold*

A large genus of some two hundred or more species widely spread over the northern hemisphere.

They are mostly herbaceous perennials, many with characteristic rhizometous rootstock or corms, sword-like leaves, and flowers of exquisite beauty and colouring. It is the seed-heads and fine leaves that are of value for the dried flower arranger—especially the leaves, which are such a splendid foil to the other round-type foliage. Should the leaves be too long or too wide, they can easily be trimmed to scale with fine-bladed scissors.

The native British *I. fœtidissima* (Gladwin, Gladdon, Stinking Iris or Roast Beef Plant—so called from the peculiar odour emitted by the leaves if bruised) is found growing wild in deciduous woodlands and thickets on chalky soils, but the keen collector would do well to cultivate it, if possible, in order to harvest in abundance the dark seed-pods which, when bursting, display fantastic orange-scarlet globular seeds. These opening seed-pods can be varnished (page 66) but will always need gentle handling.

Another of the native British irises, this time found growing wild in marshland or low down by river banks, is *I. Pseudacorus* (the Yellow Flag Iris, or Sword Flag) with beautiful striped leaves. Its bright yellow flowers are veined like those of the pale mauve *I. fœtidissima*, and it is this species which is reputed to be the emblematic fleur-de-lis of France.

Among the cultivated bearded class should be mentioned *I. pallida dalmatica*, especially for its leaves which remain so usefully green until almost the end of the year. The *argentea* (silver-striped) and *aurea* (gold-striped) forms are a must for the leaf gatherer. The seed-heads of *I. Xiphium* (the Spanish Iris) are especially adaptable for drying, and so also are those of the earlier flowering Dutch strain.

All irises welcome shallow planting, so that their roots can be baked by the sun. Unless divided every few years, they grow together in a tight waterproof mass, so much so that in some of the poorer parts of Turkey the peasant folk use them as roof-coverings for shelter rather than for show.

In ancient history, the iris, called after the messenger of the gods—the rainbow was her bridge, linking earth and heaven so that she could carry the messages of the immortals down to mortal men—was greatly valued, both for its beauty (its rainbow variety of colours won it its name) and for its medicinal and cosmetic uses. In *Flowers in History*, Peter Coats mentions the Pharaoh Thutmosis I, who so greatly prized his collection of medicinal herbs, roots and seeds, brought back in 1950 B.C. from the Syrian wars, that he caused a likeness of the iris to be carved on a marble panel which can still be seen in the Ammon Temple at Karnak. Mediaeval ladies used orris (iris) root in the ointments which they rubbed into their hands and cheeks. The recipe for "Surrup of Long Life" on page 148 contains "blew Flower de Lis".

In spite of the confusion through the centuries as to whether the iris or the lily was the heraldic fleur-de-lis, or fleur-de-luce, of France, it seems clear that the iris flower, with its three stamens (the lily has twice as many), was the true one. It is generally held, furthermore, that the native British water-flag, *I. Pseudacorus*, was the one adopted by Louis VII—the fleur-de-Louis—as his symbol during the Crusades, and thereafter proclaimed the fleur-de-lis of France. In *Henry VI*, Shakespeare dramatises the protracted wars between France and England which followed Henry V's death, after his conquest of a large portion of the French realm had made him regent of France—a conquest his baby son could not hold:

> *Sad tidings bring I to you out of France*
> *Of loss, of slaughter, and discomfiture . . .*
> *Awake, awake, English nobility!*
> *Let not sloth dim your honours new-begot:*
> *Cropt are the flower-de-luces in your arms;*
> *Of England's coat one half is cut away.*

Notwithstanding this setback, the fleur-de-lis was incorporated in the English Royal Standard until the reign of George III, and today still has a place in St Edward's Crown, and in the Imperial Crown.

In the Language of Flowers, the iris has many meanings: faith, wisdom and valour; hope, light and power; eloquence, message of promise; herb of the moon; and, when bestowed on a man, good luck gift.

*LAPSANA——L. communis——Compositæ——*NIPPLEWORT
No dried material arranger can afford to be without ample pickings of this composite, which appears in almost all the arrangements illustrated in this book. An admitted weed in the garden,

it is highly decorative and full of growth in the hedgerow. As it is found in flower for many months of the year, its harvesting period is conveniently a very long one. It should not be gathered until the flowers are just over and the slender, much-branched panicles of delicate seed-heads beginning to open. Dry flat or hanging upside down, in quantity. It will be invaluable over the years.

Nipplewort grows extensively throughout Great Britain (with the exception of northern Scotland) and in mainland Europe and Russian Asia. In earlier times it was eaten as a salad. Caesar's army once survived on this simple food "for some time"—but we are not told how long, or what the soldiers said about their rations.

LAURUS——*L. nobilis*——*Lauraceæ*——BAY

> *It serveth to adorne the house of God as well as of man; to procure warmth, comfort and strength to the limnes of men and women ... to season vessels, etc., wherein are preferred our meates, as well as our drinkes; to crowne or encircle ... the heads of the living, and to sticke and decke forth the bodies of the dead: so that from the cradle to the grave we have still use of it.*
>
> John Parkinson: *Paradisus*

Belonging to the laurel or sweet bay genus, of which it is an indispensable member, *L. nobilis* has yet had little mention in gardening books or nurserymen's catalogues. No matter: bay leaves, erstwhile conferred for deeds of valour—to be crowned with Apollo's sacred bay was, in Roman times, a tribute honouring victory—now share a culinary role with thyme and parsley and marjoram. The tree survives and flourishes in many forms, whether in tubs on the patio, terrace or balcony, or as an important ingredient of *haute cuisine*.

The glossy green leaves of this historic evergreen from the Mediterranean shores, a universal florist's delight, are most important to the dried flower arranger. Its terminal sprays and individual leaves dry easily by gentle pressing, or can be preserved by the glycerine treatment (page 63), and their enchanting shapes make them doubly valuable for small-scale arrangements. Any leaves which are surplus to requirements can enhance the flavour of tomorrow's stew!

The seventeenth century herbalist Nicholas Culpeper decreed that "neither witch nor devil, thunder nor lightning, will hurt a man where the bay tree is." So cherish your bay tree, and keep it well-fed and watered, and in return it will continue to furnish you with its exceptionally attractive and aromatic leaves.

LILIUM——*Liliaceæ*——LILY

"Consider the lilies . . . ." But where to begin? This is the symbolic flower of innocence and purity. Gabriel, the messenger from Heaven, is frequently depicted with a lily in his hand—in

Flowers Through the Ages Gabriele Tergit links the archangel's flower with the lily wands borne by English fairies. Traditionally, too, the lily has been used as an emblem of the resurrection: according to one old country custom, mourners would lay a single lily on the altar at Eastertide.

It is a large genus, renowned for its good looks, with an equally long line of outstandingly glittering cousins, such as *Fritillaria*, *Agapanthus*, *Convallaria*, *Gloriosa*, *Alstrœmeria*, *Hosta*, and the like—all of which, with many more, can be a challenge to the adventurous dried flower collector. The seed-heads of *L. auratum* (Goldband Lily) and other species are particularly valuable for drying; also those of *L. pyrenaicum* (Yellow Turk's Cap Lily) now indigenous to British woodlands and hedge-banks, especially in parts of Inverness-shire in Scotland; and in addition, *L. regale* (Royal Lily), *L. speciosum* (Showy Japanese Lily), *L. umbellatum* and its kind, and an inexhaustible number of others described in specialists' lists.

All down the ages the lily has been valued and honoured. Few flowers have so long a tradition of unchanging beauty and fragrance. So may the dried flower arranger of today and tomorrow continue to incorporate in his work this fair symbol of purity and light—this shining symbol of peace.

MAHONIA——*Berberidaceæ*

No garden or shrubbery can be complete without some members of this family; neither should the collector lack a stock for his arrangements. The magnificent sprays of pinnate leaves with large terminal leaflets, glossy and later in the year reddish in colour, become the glory of the dried leaf store. Those of the Japanese *M. japonica* and the Chinese *M. Bealei* are the most spectacular. Press them fairly hard, as they may be tough and pressure-resistant; the results are most rewarding. *M. Aquifolium*, the common Barberry species, which successfully frequents shrub plantings or game coverts, has good leaves which turn scarlet late in the year. Though there is at present no supporting evidence to go on, experiment with silica gel treatment on some of the exquisite early-flowering racemes of blooms might bring good results.

MATRICARIA——*M. eximia*, syn. *Chrysanthemum Parthenium*——*Compositæ*——FEVERFEW
   Fryed with a little wyne and oyl in a frying pan and applied warm outwardly to the
   places, it helpeth the wind and Cholik in the lower part of the Belly.

Nicholas Culpeper: *Herball*

A native of the Caucasus: the garden double and dwarf forms of "Ball's Double White" and "Golden Ball"—a lemon yellow—are the best to grow. They dry well if picked just before or at their prime, and hung upside down.

While on the subject of the *Matricaria* genus, and its kinsman *Chamomilla* (Chamomile), it is worth keeping an eye open for its relatives growing wild on farm cart-tracks and in waste places. Their flower-heads should dry as easily as those of their upper-class cousins in herbaceous border or parterre display, and some of their pretty, finely dissected, mature leaves could be pressed.

MOLUCELLA——*M. lævis*——*Labiatæ*——BELLS OF IRELAND, SHELL FLOWER, MOLUCCA BALM

Surely there is no more lovely or exciting plant for the dried material collector to seek. *M. lævis* is a beautiful green garden half-hardy annual, with pale cup-shaped calyces. They dry silvery-fawn if picked when ripe and hung upside down. They also respond well to the glycerine treatment (pages 63-66) but—alas—are not always easy to grow; and consequently it is difficult to guarantee successful harvesting. Their beauty and usefulness to the dried flower arranger, however, make it well worth-while expending every effort, from year to year, in order to give them their somewhat erratic cultural requirements. The best way to secure even partial success is to plant out the seedlings in groups in different parts of the garden, and hope for the best. They appear in Fig. 19 on page 65.

Though molucella looks at its best in tall arrangements, smaller pieces—especially the flower tips—can be very effective when trimmed and cut to scale.

MONARDA——*M. didyma* syn. *M. coccinea*——*Labiatæ*——SWEET BERGAMOT, OSWEGO TEA, BEE BALM, HORSEMINT

This summer-flowering, deliciously aromatic perennial enhances any herbaceous border with its deep red flowers. For the dried flower arranger, too, it is invaluable, with erect stems and rounded whorls of seed-heads. It should be picked as the petals fall, then dried lying flat and stored in like manner.

By the middle of the eighteenth century, it was being sold plentifully in Covent Garden Market in London, the seeds having been collected and imported from Oswego on Lake Ontario, where the leaves were used for making tea. It was for a long time relegated to the kitchen or herb garden, its leaves being in demand for flavouring. Later, happily, it was re-prieved and given, as it should be, a place of importance in the herbaceous border, alongside its fragrant relatives. The genus was named after a Spanish physician, Nicolas Monarda, whose writings were translated into English in 1577, under the title *Joyfull Newes out of the newe founde worlde wherein is declared the rare and singular vertues of diverse and sundrie Herbes.*

MUSCARI——*Liliaceæ*——GRAPE HYACINTH

Considering its small stature, surely few small bulbous plants have such a string of names as this one: grape hyacinth, starch hyacinth, feathered hyacinth, musk hyacinth, tassel hyacinth —the last name being the most charmingly apt.

This native of the Mediterranean region is certainly one of the gems of the spring bulb world, and very easy of culture. For the dried material collector its pale, fragile, ethereal seed-heads are beyond compare, and should be harvested with the greatest care on a dry day, after flowering is over. Once dry, they can be gently laid flat in a florist's box, stacked in layers for use when needed. For assembly, it will be necessary to insert wires in the hollow brittle stems. The seed-heads should be lightly tapped to disperse the little black seeds. In addition to *M. armeniacum*, *M. azureum*, *M. botryoides* and *M. tubergenianum*, which are all invaluable for the collector, bulb catalogues list many others which would, no doubt, be charming and useful.

NARCISSUS——*Amaryllidaceæ*

Being stamped with the meale of cockle and honie, it draweth forth thornes and stubs out of any part of the bodie.

John Gerard: *Herball*

Legend sadly relates that the beautiful young Narcissus, son of the nymph Leiriope, was so pampered by the nymphs in his youth that he became devoured by egotism and conceit, and heartlessly scorned all who fell in love with him. The goddess Artemis punished him by causing him to fall in love, yet denying him any opportunity to satisfy his desire: for he fell in love with his own reflection, and idled away his waking hours by the waterside, contemplating, in enchantment, the beautiful image in the water and falling deeper and deeper in love with himself. One legend holds that he slipped beneath the water and was drowned, and that on his arrival in the world of the dead, Nemesis, the goddess of vengeance, sent him back to earth as a narcissus flower (*Narcissus poeticus*) so that he could continue nodding at his own watery image for ever after; the Fates, however, arranged that the flower's scent should be so sweet as to cause madness—a perpetual reminder of his punishment. Robert Graves quotes a second version, which relates how, desperate with love, Narcissus plunged a dagger into his heart; as his blood soaked into the earth, so the white narcissus flowers sprang up by the waterside, each with a corolla rimmed with blood-red in his memory.

The narcissus referred to by the ancient Greeks was probably the beautiful *N. Tazetta* or bunched type. A legend, quoted by Alice Coats, holds that it was originally white, but that when Dis came upon Persephone in her flowery meadow she was sleeping with a wreath of them in her hair and the pure white petals turned yellow at his touch, as he carried her off into the underworld; and so, happily, today we have both white and yellow snub-nose (small cup) species, such as *N. poeticus*, *N. Tazetta*, *N. incomparabilis*, *N. Jonquilla*, *N. triandrus*, and other small forms—and the doubles. In addition, there is the trumpet daffodil, scorned by the herbalists for many centuries and called "Bastard Daffodil", and other degrading names. "It is needlesse," said John Parkinson, "to spend a great deale of time and labour upon such smally respected flowers but that in the beholding of them we may therein admire the worke of the

Creatour who can frame such diversity in one thing." Gerard, writing earlier, in 1597, was also casual about them: "The common yellow Daffodilly or Daffadowndilly is so well knowne to all that it needeth no description."

The dried flower arranger can preserve all varieties of the snub-nose, flat-flowered kinds in silica gel incredibly easily, and they will retain their delicate colour with superb success. To list them would be superfluous—the nurseryman, the bulb specialist, the florist, the market-stall-holder, the street barrow boy, all have them in bewildering quantities. The wild species are mostly to be found in Mediterranean regions, and many are indigenous to the Iberian peninsula. In Britain, *N. biflorus* (Primrose Peerless), growing wild, is regarded as a garden escape—"Most common in our country gardens, generally knowne every where," said Gerard. When preserving, whichever species or variety is used, individual flower-heads should be wired singly and placed, preferably face downwards, in the preserving agent, for some three to six days; then if some are found to be too limp to the touch, they can be re-immersed for a longer drying. This is one of the many occasions when the dried material worker has to play it by feel—yes, and by ear too, tuning in to a subtlety of sound—a skill which is soon acquired by practice.

In spite of the centuries of its existence, few medicinal uses were found for it. Turner held that "the roote broken with a little hony maketh the cut synewes to grow together agayn if it be layd to them plasterwyse"; and Gerard quoted the Greek physician Galen as saying that narcissus could be used to "glue" together great wounds, and Plutarch as saying that the flower got its name because it "did benum the sinewes and cause drowsinesse".

N. Tazetta, the original (daffodil) type is known to have been growing in the eastern world—in Syria, Persia, Kashmir, China and Japan—in about A.D. 1000. Double forms were in cultivation about two hundred years later; and later still came the out-of-this-world, somewhat tender frailty, "Paper-White", with its heaven-sent fragrance.

Together with other historically famous flowers, narcissus was wont to take part sometimes in a little game of cheating, described by Peter Coats in his *Flowers in History*. It appears in bouquets in flower paintings from the earliest ages, together with such ever-populars as irises, roses and tulips—not forgetting the extra fancies such as butterflies, beetles, house-flies, ladybirds and dewdrops. It does not take long to conclude that, in view of the different flowering seasons involved, the artist solved his problem by keeping a carefully selected file of the plant prototypes for use when needed—such artist's licence being, perhaps, not unlike that which this book advocates for the dried arranger's store!

NIGELLA——*Ranunculaceæ*——FENNEL FLOWER

This is a small genus of hardy, decorative, summer-flowering annuals, with finely cut, fennel-like leaves, grown for garden ornament. It was cultivated in English gardens in Gerard's time.

The aromatic seeds were used medicinally and, in France—where they are known as *quatre-épices* or *toute-épice*—for flavouring.

N. damascena (the blue Love-in-a-Mist) is the most commonly grown, but some of the hybrid flowers are white—"Persian Jewels"—and pink—"Persian Rose". It is a native of the Mediterranean regions and West Asia, and is a very attractive addition to the dried store. Nigella seed-heads are of unique value to the dried material collector, with their parchment-coloured globular seed-capsules looking like lanterns striped in purple. They will be ready for harvesting in late summer, and should be stripped of most of their green whiskers, dried on their own stems, and preferably varnished.

In the Language of Flowers it indicates perplexity.

OLEARIA, syn. *SHAWIA*——*Compositæ*——DAISY BUSH, TREE DAISY
A large tender family with beautiful evergreen leaves resembling those of the olive, and not-so-exciting daisy-like flowers: they mostly emanate from Australia and New Zealand. Daisies are of lowly stature and, as Alice Coats remarks, quoting Mr A. B. Anderson, it is surprising to see them flowering up there on the branches; reasonable enough in the Antipodes "where everything is naturally upside-down" but distracting in England, where Chaucer's beloved "day's-eye" is expected to shine out from the grass.

Among the hardies are *O. Haastii*, a nine-foot-high bushy shrub with dark shining green leaves, glabrous above and white-felted beneath, and hawthorn-like nondescript flowers; and *O. macrodonta*, a seaside semi-tree which has very decorative leathery leaves with toothed margins and much more spectacular clusters of white flowers with yellow centres. The leaves of both should be treasured and preserved, either by pressing or in glycerine. It could be worth experimenting in preserving the flower-heads of *O. macrodonta* by silica gel treatment, although this has not yet been tried. A beautiful hybrid, *O. scilloniensis*, introduced to the famous Tresco Abbey gardens in the Isles of Scilly by Captain A. A. Dorrien-Smith in 1910, has grey leaves and lavender-purple flowers.

PÆONIA——*Ranunculaceæ*——PÆONY
Syrupe made of the flowers of Peionie helpeth greatly the Falling Sickness.

John Gerard: *Herball*

One of the most ancient and beautiful of plants, steeped in legend and symbolism. Gerard quotes one of the old superstitions about its harvesting, culled from Apuleius: "The seeds or graines of Peionie shine in the night time like a candle . . . of necessitie it must be gathered in the night; for if any man shall pluck off the fruit in the day time, being seene of the Woodpecker, he is in danger to lose his eies"—but he adds, with the air of a serious botanist dismissing a trifle, "All these things be most vaine and frivolous."

The paeony comes of a large family, now divided mainly into three groups: herbaceous, perennials and their species, and, most important of all, the tree paeony—one of the most glorious and impressive of all shrubs. The smaller of the double species herbaceous flowers preserve very successfully in a drying agent; the leaves, pointed and much divided, press well; and some of the seed-heads, too, are worth collecting. The greatest treasure, however, is to be found in the beautifully veined, and quite superlatively coloured, divided foliage of the tree paeony. The beauty of the leaves is such that they make pictures on their own in an arrange-ment, and once they have been seen, no other foliage can compare with them.

Press as many of these abundantly spraying, rich beauties as you dare to collect without harming the tree—leave them on their own firm stalks, and cherish them as the most precious of leaves in your keeping. It might be worth treating some of the leaves—the larger ones—by the total immersion glycerine preserving method described on pages 63-66. Any varieties of tree paeony from China—*P. suffruticosa,* syn. *P. arborea,* or *P. Moutan*—will be worth growing or seeking at least for the leaves, though the smaller flowers should be chosen in double form from herbaceous border types, such as *P. officinalis* and its kindred species. These are listed in detail in specialist nurserymen's catalogues and displayed magnificently at flower shows. The native English *P. mascula* is found growing in rock clefts at Steep Holme in the Bristol Channel, and is believed to have been brought there in the Middle Ages by the monks.

In the Language of Flowers these brilliant blooms represent bashfulness or shame.

PAPAVER——*Papaveraceæ*——POPPY

> *Or on a half-reap'd furrow sound asleep,*
> *Drows'd with the fume of poppies, while thy hook*
> *Spares the next swathe and all its twined flowers—*
>
> John Keats: *To Autumn*

For centuries poppy flowers have symbolised sleep and forgetfulness; now, with a change of fate, they have also become a national symbol of remembrance.

We associate poppies with cornfields, and they have been blooming there, among the crops, since prehistoric times. Persephone, the daughter of Demeter—goddess of the cornfields—was carried off by Dis, the god of the underworld, while gathering flowers in a meadow; and angry and sorrowing, her mother swore that the fields should remain barren until the girl was restored. Zeus accordingly promised that Dis should give up Persephone, providing only that she had not yet tasted the food of the dead. But Persephone had picked a pomegranate in the orchards of the underworld and had eaten its scarlet seeds. The gods therefore agreed that she should spend six months of each year in the realm of Dis—the dark winter months, when

Demeter grieves for her daughter—and six months with her mother. When Persephone is restored to Demeter each springtime, the corn begins to thrust its way up from the earth; but when the harvest is over, the girl is borne away again for her yearly sleep in the underworld. The scarlet-flowering, scarlet-seeded pomegranate is at once a symbol of death and a promise of resurrection. The Roman poet Ovid describes how Persephone was gathering poppies when Dis stole her away—their brilliant scarlet promising her eventual resurrection from her sleep among the dead—and the famous gold ring from the Mycenae Treasure portrays Demeter bestowing three poppy-heads on her daughter.

Without any doubt poppy seed-heads, with all their muted colours, with their diverse sizes and shapes, and with no two markings alike, can provide unique and quite superlative components for the most exclusive, as well as the most comprehensive, store. They are a beautiful feature of one of the assemblies illustrated on page 48. Celia Thaxter once remarked that she knew no other flower that was so charming and picturesque. "The stalks often take a curve, a twist from a current of air or some impediment, and the fine stems will turn and twist in all sorts of graceful ways, but the drooping bud is always held erect when the time comes for it to blossom"—and indeed, to seed. A poppy, moreover, being of a tidy mind, will always throw away its calyx once it blossoms. What more can the dried collector ask for?

The seed-heads can be harvested with ease throughout late summer and early autumn—and dreary dampness does not affect them unduly. Strip them of leaves, grade them in sizes, and dry them on their own strong stems, flat, in boxes, so that the abundant black seeds are not lost. Among the cultivated types, *P. Rhœas* (the Corn Poppy) in all its double forms, especially the begonia-flowered, and *P. somniferum* (the Opium Poppy), symbol of sleep, carnation-flowered and paeony-flowered, are some of the most impressive seed-head producers. Seedsmen's catalogues list a number of others—and all are hardy annuals and easy to grow. Many, too, can be found growing wild, wherever they can survive the ever-increasing scourge of chemical weed-killers. Seed-heads of the cultivated herbaceous garden subject *P. orientale* can also be of use, though they are larger and coarser, and have thicker stems than the annual varieties, and are more suitable for larger arrangements. Ruskin's version of Lindley's writings is not amiss: "I muse over the seed-heads, those supremely graceful urns (sometimes thought of as pew ends) that are wrought with such matchless elegance of shape, and thank whatever strange power they hold within."

Papaver is a large genus, being found all over the world, with many uses and many names. The herbalists and country folk called the poppy "Headache" and "Headworke" from its effect; "If a man take to much of it, it is hurtfull," Turner warned, "for it taketh a mannis memori away and killeth hym." Parkinson, who welcomed the beautiful garden varieties, gave a curious country name for the poppy—Joan Silver Pin, which is apparently derived from an East Anglian nickname for a single bright article shining out unexpectedly from a mass of dirt. The farmers used to call the common field poppy their Corn Rose, but they had other, less agreeable names for it—Canker Rose, and Redweed: no wonder, considering its ability to sprout afresh after lying dormant for years. "With us it groweth much amongst the rye and barley," Turner remarked. The French call the poppy *coquelicot*—for according to legend, on hearing a cock crow the poppy moves as though her name were called; to the Germans it is *Klatschrose*—the tell-tale rose.

The Language of Flowers variously calls the poppy courage, time, silence, consolation and wild extravagance—it seems, indeed, that all forms of existence owe something to this flower.

PHLOMIS——*Labiatæ*

Being stamped with salt and applied, it cureth the biting of a mad dogge.

John Gerard: Herball

Though these perennial herbs, or low shrubs, are described as tough and coarse-growing, they are nevertheless most distinctive and lend their surroundings an air which is subtly different from that of neighbouring plants. They revel in sunny, light-soiled positions, and may easily be cut back to ground level in a hard winter. *P. viscosa*, syn. *P. Russeliana*, from Syria, bears its yellow flowers in whorls, which produce fascinating seed-heads—terribly exciting for the dried flower collector. So also does *P. samia* from Greece, and above all the evergreen shrub *P. fruticosa* (Jerusalem Sage) to be found growing abundantly in the Mediterranean region.

Many leaves of the phlomis tribe are slightly white and woolly, and should not be stripped from the stems but allowed to dry naturally. Dry phlomis plants by hanging them upside down or laying them flat. They dry quickly, and the seed-heads make unique material for placing in the centre and low down in dried arrangements.

PLANTAGO——*Plantaginaceæ*——PLANTAIN

P. major (the Great Plantain) grows mostly in large groups on common ground—in the front of hedgerows and on the edge of fields and pathways—and flowers from May onwards. Its long green and brown seed-heads should be picked in all stages of growth, and certainly well before they show signs of running to seed. Pick in quantity—all lengths and shapes—and varnish immediately. Lay the varnished heads flat on sheets of paper to dry (change the paper as need arises until the varnish has dried). Store lying flat in open boxes.

P. lanceolata (the Ribwort Plantain) has a much smaller head, but is useful for smaller arrangements, as also is *P. media* (the Hoary Plantain, Lamb's Tongue) frequently found growing on chalky soils. In fact, all plantains are worth collecting and preserving.

POTENTILLA——*Rosaceæ*

P. Anserina (Silver-weed), a humble cinquefoil wildling of the illustrious Rosaceae tribe, is a silky prostrate perennial, found growing widespread and common in damp, grassy and waste spaces, and indeed across the continent of Europe and in Asia. Its main, and very important, claim to attention is its quite exquisite silver foliage, with well-toothed leaflets, alternately large and small, which are sometimes silvery on both sides, sometimes just on the underside, sometimes on neither side—but never on the upper side only!

The delicate leaves with their beautiful silvery iridescence should be gathered, if possible, in quantity, and *kept flat* from the moment of picking—otherwise they tend to curl. Pressed dry and stored between sheets of blotting paper until use, they form an enchanting base and outline for many a small arrangement.

It may well be exciting for the keen collector to look out for other cinquefoil potentillas, and also for *Fragaria vesca* (the Wild Strawberry) all of which have fantastically beautifully shaped and coloured leaves.

PRIMULA——Primulaceæ

> *The dried of fielde Primrose gathered in Autumne and given to drink in ale purgeth*
> *by vomite very forcibly waterish humours Choler and Flegme.*
>
> John Gerard: *Herball*

The alpine *P. Auricula* and some of the other cultivated and wild species form clustered seed-heads worth watching for. These make out-of-the-ordinary decorative features for small flat arrangements, but should not be gathered until they are fully formed.

Auriculas—aristocrats of the *Primula* family—are divided into two main groups. The Show varieties, whether pampered treasures or hobby plants, are shrouded in a certain mystery, for they require mainly green-house treatment—not on account of their tenderness but because their make-up runs! They are heavily powdered with a farina coating about the "eyes", heads, leaves and stems, and need protection, therefore, from the devastating effect of even a minor April shower. Some of the seed-heads make fascinating dried material, though it is seldom that their proud owners will part with the rare, exotic seed.

Alternatively, the collector may be well advised to watch out for seed-heads of the cultivated primrose and polyantha cousins, provided, always, the sparrows have not got in first!

*PRUNUS——P. Laurocerasus——Rosaceæ——*COMMON LAUREL, CHERRY LAUREL

> *. . . is well respected for the beauty of the leaves and their lasting or continuall greenness.*
>
> John Gerard: *Herball* (1633)
>
> *Laurel is green for a season and love is sweet for a day.*
>
> A. C. Swinburne: *Hymn to Proserpine*

Essentially enshrined in garlands, wreaths and crowns commemorating deeds of valour, the laurel has played a noble part since ancient times. It was sacred to Apollo, and thus associated with poesy and prophecy. In the laurel groves of Tempe, Apollo was purified after he killed the Python—the great serpent of Delphi; and each eighth year, at the Pythian festival, this legend was re-enacted—a boy fled from Delphi to Tempe, and was brought back with triumphal song, garlanded with laurel. The Greeks awarded a laurel crown to the winner of the Pythian games, and in Roman times the wreath bestowed on victorious commanders was formed of laurel or of bay (the sweet laurel, or bay, is described on page 126). Laurel leaves were laid under a sleeper's pillow to invoke inspiration; and the Pythoness—the priestess of the Delphic Oracle—chewed laurel leaves in the oracular ritual. In later years the laurel has come to be regarded as a symbol of victory and peace. Notwithstanding its renown, current records seem singularly unimaginative when describing this most estimable member of a glorious family. It seems indeed to be regarded as an ugly duckling, not worthy of more than the barest mention.

Belonging to a vast and varying clan, this invaluable evergreen—the common or cherry laurel—has come to be taken for granted. It grows to a height of twenty feet, and is a useful windbreak or screen for covert planting. Long may it remain so, for it is extremely valuable to the dried material collector. The leaves in all their shapes and sizes (so long as not picked when immature) form, with those of the rhododendron, the absolute basis of the dried material store. It is important for the collector to ensure that secateurs, and not those lethal hedge clippers, are used when laurel is trimmed or pruned—though this suggestion may not generally be wholly popular with the gardener! Gather the leaves abundantly—large and small. They press easily, retaining their green colour, and last for years. They can be given the glycerine treatment if desired (pages 63-66), and it might also be possible to skeletonise them (page 157). Some of the terminal sprays form delightful dried material.

The common or cherry laurel comes from Eastern Europe and Asia Minor, and flowers prettily and fragrantly in springtime. There are a number of species, which include its kinsman *P. lusitanica* (the Portugal Laurel).

In the Language of Flowers laurel means glory—unless it be in flower, when it implies perfidy.

*PRUNUS——P. lusitanica, syn. P. azorica——Rosaceæ——*PORTUGAL LAUREL
> *All these Plants are violent purges and therefore great caution is to be had in the use of them.*
>
> *Old Herball*

This hawthorn-scented evergreen from the Iberian peninsula provides the dried arranger with some of his most basic and quite invaluable sprays and individual leaves. Branches can be preserved by the glycerine treatment (pages 63-66) or small sprays and single leaves pressed. Its slender dark glossy green leaves, finely toothed and red-stalked, can be harvested at any time, so long as they are mature, and no effort should be spared in seeking out a means to ensure a constant supply. When dried, the leaves turn a wonderfully glowing, dark brown colour, and retain much of their original shine. If stored carefully—between sheets of blotting paper—and with no suspicion of a damp atmosphere, they should form an indispensable component of the store. They form a glossy, dark background to the centrepiece in Fig. 14 on page 48.

RUMEX——Polygonaceæ——DOCK, SORREL

Many of these wild docks and sorrels dry well for decoration. Their whorl-shaped seed-heads—lime-green early in the season, but dark red later—are most useful and decorative (they appear, for example, in two of the assemblies illustrated on page 48). There are many varieties growing in pasture and waste land, but only the more delicate forms should be gathered. Hang them upside down to dry, and pull the sprays apart as required. Once dried and carefully stored, they will last for years.

Rumex is a fair-sized genus, with such species as spinach-rhubarb from Abyssinia, Great Water Dock, and Herb Patience—a native of North America. As a herb it plays its part in medicine—particularly *R. obtusifolius* (the Butter Dock) which relieves nettle-sting by its tannin anti-irritant qualities. Happily, as any child should know, Nature has thoughtfully arranged that the two plants usually grow near one another.

In the Language of Flowers the dock means patience.

RUTA——Rutaceæ——RUE

We may call it herb o' grace o' Sundays:
O, you must wear your rue with a difference.

William Shakespeare: *Hamlet*

The captivating rue, or herb of grace, an erstwhile member of the ancient medicinal herb gardens, is a kinsman of such treasures as citrus, choisya, skimmia, and many other notable plants. In the Language of Flowers, it is cruelly portrayed as disdain—but why? Could a gloriously cheerful drift of rue, such as *R. graveolens* "Jackman's Blue", with delicate filigree foliage and iridescent hues on every leaf, be indifferent to the effect of its charm—or the loving care of its admirers?

These pretty leaves are difficult to preserve, alas, although the greenish-yellow, insignificant flowers produce fragile seed-heads which jut out from its sprays of leaves. These dry easily and are long-lasting.

SALVIA——Labiatæ——SAGE

And what an abundance of herbs, shrubs and sub-shrubs the family provides—both cultivated and wild—historical, ornamental, culinary, medicinal, fragrant in leaf, colourful in flower, and ethereal in seed-head. What more can man presume to cull from just one tribe of treasures? Its favourite, and maybe now somewhat derelict home, is the kitchen garden. Some extra-special species may well have survived there from yester-year, and the collector may have to tussle with a tangle of goosegrass, ground elder and bramble, to extricate the invaluable victim of neglect.

For dried arrangement purposes, it is the seed-heads which are important—beautiful, delicate spikes of seed-capsules arranged in whorls or in racemes on a characteristic squared tapering stem. These withstand winter weather and need not necessarily be harvested in haste. (They appear in Fig. 13 on page 40). Gather with a good length of stem and retain some of the sweet-smelling leaves—kitchen permitting! They require little drying—just an upright or lying position, until needed for use.

The *Salvia* genus is very prolific, and many species are now difficult to locate, but the collector will find all he needs among those growing in the herbaceous border, and above all in the old-fashioned herb-garden. Moreover, his interest, being centred on the seed-heads, will not conflict with the gourmet's culinary needs.

In the Language of Flowers the sages have had much attention—as indeed so charming a tribe should. Sage symbolises esteem, domestic virtue, and expressions such as "I think of you" and "Forever thine".

SCROPHULARIA——*Scrophulariaceæ*——FIGWORT
There are a number of species, both cultivated and wild. Related to the penstemon kindred, these are statuesque in growth, with characteristic square stems, which dry well and soon lose their not-so-nice smell. They are mostly moisture- and shade-loving. The garden species *S. nodosa* (Knotted Figwort) and its beautiful variegated form are both attractive and useful, but the one of real value to the dried plant collector is *S. aquatica* (Water Figwort, Bishop's Leaves), found growing on damp pond-sides. This has large leaves for pressing, and very fine dull panicles of flowers, which dry into superb candelabra-like clusters of seed-heads, so decorative in outlining arrangements, and which last for years. Dried figwort seed-heads appear at the centre back of the frontispiece assembly.

SILENE——*S. Cucubalus*——*Caryophyllaceæ*——BLADDER CAMPION
Growing wild in pastures and waste land, particularly on the sunny side of a hedgerow, this much-branched wild flower has seed-heads which are quite invaluable for drying—indeed, it is well worth cultivating from seed specially for dried material harvesting. It appears in many of the assemblies illustrated in this book, among them Fig. 19 on page 65.

The beautiful egg-shaped seed-heads should be harvested when open in mid-August, as soon as the flowers are over and the seed-heads fully formed. Pick when dry, if possible, gathering sprays with as much stalk as possible because their slender stems do not lend themselves easily to wiring. Varnish immediately and spread out on paper to dry (renewing the paper every few hours to prevent the fragile sprays from sticking to it). Once dry, store flat in open boxes, spread out loosely. Varnished sprays of bladder campion seed-heads provide the dried material arranger with fantastically beautiful wherewithal for adding unique and interesting lightness to an arrangement's outer edges, and for drooping over the rim of the container.

Silene, and its garden forms of *Lychnis*, make up a vast tribe, and the species vary in size and character considerably—some being alpines, and others herbaceous or wild. It is also related to *Agrostemma*, which is described on page 104.

The campions have had various names throughout their long history: White Ben, Spatling Rose, Knap-bottle (from its shape, and the snap that the calyx makes if squeezed in the fingers), Witch's Thimble, Gardener's Delight, Ragged Robin, Cuckoo Flower, Gardener's Eye, Meadow Pink; *L. Coronaria* is the Rose Campion; *L. chalcedonica* is the Flower of Bristow, the Flower of Constantinople—rather more far-flung—and Cross of Jerusalem. With such a background, no wonder that our lovely little wildling stands out in its charm and produces such superb seed-heads for preserving.

The dried flower collector would do well to watch out along the coastal shore in the north-east and the south of England, and in quarries in Kent, for other varieties of this treasure plant, as they all have superlative and delicate seed-heads, so perfect for drying.

Like the august laurel, the bladder campion was once thought to be a charm against thunder and lightning; so the dried flower collector who gathers it from the hedgerows is providing himself with an amulet as well as with treasured material.

SPIRÆA——*Rosaceæ*

A large genus of deciduous shrubs and herbaceous perennials, with an ancient Greek name meaning "a plant for garlands". (There is considerable confusion between these garden perennials and the saxifrage genus of *Astilbe* seen in so many hybrid forms growing in moist or partial shade, with lofty inflorescence—the last word in poise, grace and elegance. Not only are the leaves good for pressing, but the mahogany stems and seed-heads are worth preserving.)

Returning to spiraea, there is the handsome arching, July-flowering shrub *Holodiscus discolor*, syn. *S. ariæfolia* from North America, with feathery, cream, lace-like flower panicles—so good for drying. The leaves, slightly hairy on the underside, press well. Of the herbaceous forms, *Filipendula Ulmaria*, syn. *S. Ulmaria* (Queen of the Meadow—the native British wild Meadowsweet) is as beautiful as it is invaluable, both for its flowers and its leaves. It is to be found in Britain and throughout Europe, Asia and North America, on the edges of ponds and in damp ditches. *S. Aruncus*, syn. *Aruncus sylvester* (Goat's Beard) is another outstanding plant to look for.

SYRINGA——Oleaceæ——LILAC

Syringa is so named from the Greek word *syrinx*, "a tube", referring to the shape of the flowers. It is the seed-heads which are of importance to the dried material collector, especially those of the common *S. vulgaris*, and other single-flowered varieties, with their graceful panicles, which dry perfectly while still on the tree and need not be harvested until late summer. Most of the modern double species are apt to produce seed-heads which are somewhat too dense and heavy, though these can be trimmed and thinned out according to requirements. They should either be stored standing upright or lying flat in a box.

Lilacs mostly emanate from China, Japan, Persia and south-eastern Europe.

The name "syringa" is sometimes misapplied to *Philadelphus* (Mock Orange), which, in spite of its beauty and fragrance, is of little use in dried work.

TAGETES——Compositæ——MARIGOLD

Some use to make their heyre yelow with the floure of this herbe, not being content with the natural colour which God hath given them.

William Turner: *Herball*

A native of Mexico and Argentina, *T. patula* (known as the French Marigold) is not to be confused with the native British wild bur, corn marigold or marsh marigold, which would be unsuitable for the dried flower collector. Many of the innumerable *Tagetes*—hardy, half-hardy and modern hybrids—are now listed in seed catalogues, and are well worth growing for drying, especially the African and French marigolds of recent introduction. The fully double and somewhat quilled forms dry best, and when dried, the paler yellow retain a clearer shade than the bronze, red and orange colours. The flower-heads should be put on false wire stems in order to overcome as much as possible the pungent smell of the stalks. They should be immersed in the chemical crystals for several days, as described on pages 61-63.

In the Language of Flowers the French marigold is the flower of jealousy, and the marigold itself means prediction or uneasiness. The African marigold means a vulgar mind.

TIARELLA——Saxifragaceæ——FALSE MITREWORT

These hardy herbaceous evergreen shade-loving plants impart gaiety wherever they are seen, whether they are growing in the wild garden, the herbaceous border, or anywhere else in the garden, and they are perfect ground-cover for the gardener. This in itself is a good thing for the collector, as there is plenty to choose from among the dense mass of very pleasing heart-shaped, lobed leaves—sometimes with marbled markings and beautiful autumn tints. *T. cordifolia* (the Foam Flower) from North America, with its enchanting white flowers, is very cheerful and attractive—and its leaves are superb. The wavy-toothed, variegated leaves of *T. polyphylla* from the Himalayas are also worth collecting, as no doubt are other members of this family, which should be sought for.

Being somewhat wavy and indented, the leaves will need gentle, careful handling and drying, over a long period of some three to four weeks, according to their age and condition. The green, bronze and reddish leaves of *T. wherryi* from the south-east of the United States of America may take even longer to dry, as they will be gathered later in the season. Because the leaves are slightly hairy a watch must be kept against mildew while drying, and the sheets of blotting paper may require changing from time to time. The most effective precaution against this hazard is to gather in dry weather.

TULIPA——*Liliaceæ*——TULIP, TURK'S CAP

> *There is lately a flower . . . a Toolip, which has engrafted the love and affection of most people into it, and what is this Toolip? A well-complexioned stink, an ill savour wrapped up in elegant colours.*
>
> <div align="right">Thomas Fuller: <i>Speech of Flowers</i> (1660)</div>

> *Those that are so mightily for the smell, may supply themselves with Perfumes, and the easier be content without this quality in this Queen of Flowers; for this might weaken or lessen her Beauty and Pleasantries. And besides, what seems to some a very pleasant smell, is by others called stinking.*
>
> <div align="right">Henry van Oosten: <i>The Dutch Gardener</i> (1703)</div>

This is a vast and strong-growing genus of spring-flowering bulbs, dating back in European history to somewhere in the mid-sixteenth century. We associate tulips with the flat, dyke-edged fields of Holland, but they came originally from the East. The *Tulipa* genus, may its name be praised, derives its name from the turban plant of Persia—the emblem of the Turkish rulers of the House of Osman. De Busbecq, the Austrian ambassador to Turkey, described them in 1554. He brought back a few plants "at great price" and planted them in his Austrian garden.

According to the herbalists, the Rose of Sharon in the Song of Songs was actually the tulip—possibly *T. sharonensis*. Gerard identified them with the lilies of the field that toiled not neither did they spin—"I do verily thinke that these are the Lillies of the field mentioned by Our Saviour . . first, their shape, for their floures resemble Lillies, and in those places whereas our Saviour was conversant they grow wilde in the fields. Secondly, the infinite varietie of colour . . . and thirdly the wondrous beautie and mixtures." Parkinson clearly delighted in them. They could be matched and planted, he said, so that the parterre in which they grew would look like "a peece of curious needle-work, or peece of painting". He remarked that they "do abide so long in their bravery"; and added, "There is no Lady or Gentlewoman of any worth that is not caught with this delight or not delighted with these flowers." Thanks be to God, there is no getting away from the ancient herbalists, however much they contradicted and spited each other in all their varying records!

The tulip mania which ensued in the seventeenth century caused the most astonishing drama in the whole history of horticulture. Exultant florists who had lucky breeding "breaks" sold their newest bulbs for fortunes. One much-quoted "price" is that fetched by a Vive le Roi bulb: two loads of wheat, four loads of rye, eight pigs, twelve fat sheep, four oxen, two hogsheads of wine, four barrels of beer, two barrels of butter, a thousand pounds of cheese, a suit of clothes and a silver cup. In *Flowers in History* Peter Coats tells another story: how a bulb farmer once ate a stew which cost him 100,000 florins—his cook had mistaken some of his rarest tulip bulbs for onions!

Critics, however, did exist; and these usually attacked the tulip for its lack of fragrance. In his *Complete Gardener's Practice*, published in 1664, Stephen Blake describes in detail a contemporary method by which gardeners hoped to bestow scent on this "stately form": one should wrap the tulip bulb in cloves, mace, cinnamon, musk and amber-grease; bury it, as usual; and water it with damask rose water. "This you may believe if you please," he wrote crisply at the end of the instructions, "but I can assure you that you will lose your labour and cost."

For the present-day gardener, selecting one or two tulips from all the multitudinous varieties is a painstaking study. "But to tell you of all the sorts of Tulipas (which are the pride of delight)," wrote Parkinson in his *Paradisus*, "they are so many, and as I may say, almost infinite, doth both passe my ability, and as I believe the skill of any other."

The beautifully formed and often transparent seed-vessels of tulip species are well worth seeking—cut their long stems (never break them) with florists' scissors to prevent bruising, and dry them flat or standing upright. Messrs Wallace & Barr, specialists of long standing on the subject of bulbs, are acknowledged authorities for lists of species to grow—*T. Clusiana* (the Lady Tulip), for instance; *T. Batalinii*; *T. linifolia*; *T. chrysantha*; *T. pulchella*; *T. violacea*; *T. tarda*, syn. *T. dasystemon*; *T. Kolpakowskiana*; *T. Eichleri*; and the *T. Greigii* species hybrids— and reference should be made to their wonderfully illustrated catalogues (their address is given on page 155). Seed-heads of the larger-flowered tulips, such as "Darwin", "Cottage", "Lily-flowered" and "Bybloemen", and many other bedding varieties can be good for drying, but any suggestion that they should be left to seed will not find favour with the honest gardener so a compromise will have to be reached; in any case, the seed-heads of the species tulips are far more attractive. The native British wild yellow *T. sylvestris* should not be overlooked.

In the Language of Flowers the red tulip utters a declaration of love, the yellow tulip one of hopeless love, and the variegated tulip—so softly—"beautiful eyes".

VIBURNUM——*Carifoliaceæ*
Besides the lovely fresh blossom so sought after for fragrance in the garden in late spring or early summer, the collector owes much to this large genus.

For leaves, there is the evergreen *V. Davidii* from China, with its broad corrugated dark green leaves which press so successfully; experiments in preserving the pretty pinkish-white flowers in silica gel might be worth a trial. Next in leaf importance is *V. rhytidophyllum*, again from China. This tall, shelter-loving evergreen has distinctive and most useful leaves—deeply wrinkled on top and fascinatingly buff-felted beneath—which can be used with either side upwards. They should be pressed really flat for some weeks, otherwise their long edges tend to curl. Again, there is *V. Tinus* (commonly known as Laurustinus) from south-eastern Europe; dark green, smaller leaves grow luxuriantly on this shrub, which should be in every garden, and are invaluable for small dried arrangements if well pressed.

And last, but no means least, there is the creamy-white May-flowering lacecap blossom of *V. Opulus* (the native English Guelder Rose or Water Elder). Beautiful as they are, they wilt quickly and will require immediate silica gel treatment lasting several days. The flowers of *V. O. sterile* (the Snowball Tree) can be similarly treated.

John Evelyn, the seventeenth century diarist and author, speaking in its praise, said, "If the medicinal properties of the leaves, bark, berries, etc., were thoroughly known, I cannot tell what our countryman would ail for which he could not find a remedy from every hedge, either for sickness or wound."

XERANTHEMUM——*Compositæ*

Unhappily this flower, much the nicest of the immortelles, does not seem to have a Christian name—the more the pity; its clumsy family name upsets its many admirers, for wherever it is seen in an arrangement it gives immense delight.

Natives of the Mediterranean region, these hardy annuals are not always to be found in seed lists—though *X. annuum* is listed and illustrated by Messrs Thompson & Morgan. Its white, purple, mauve and pink starry flowers shine enchantingly, and care should be taken when arranging to place them where they can best attract the light. Other varieties are *X. a. ligulosum*, also with double flowers—while those of *X. a. perigulosum* are described as "very double".

Without question a good supply of xeranthemum flowers should be in every arranger's collection. Unfortunately they are inclined to flower in late summer, and harvesting needs to be completed in dry weather and as soon as the flowers are open. Some of the unopened buds can be dipped in varnish, when they will make most attractive dried material. Dry the flowers on their own wiry stalks and store them standing upright or lying flat.

Part Three

PRAYER for a GRANDCHILD

Let no-one hurry her, Lord,
Give her the rare, the incomparable gift of time
Days to dream, dragonfly days, days when the
                              kingfisher
Suddenly opens for her a window on wonder.
Let no-one chivvy her, Lord; let her meander
Lark-happy through childhood, by fern-curled streams
Fringed butter-yellow with kingcups; by secret ways
That paws have worn through the wild;
Give her cuckoo-loud days and the owl's cry by
                              night.

Dear Lord, give her rainbows;
Show her a nest filled with sky-blue promises;
Scoop up the sounding oceans for her in a shell.
Let her keep her dreams,
So that she will always turn her face to the light;
Live merrily, love well;
Hold out ungloved hands to flower and child;
Be easy with animals; come to terms with time.
Lord, let her keep her dreams;
Let her riches be remembered happy days.

146

EYES AND NO EYES

WHEN THEY are still very young, may it not be that small people could be encouraged to handle growing things—something different from their brightly coloured plastic engines, Corgi cars, and objects of Outer Space. No one is ever too young to learn to hold a daisy, and to love it—to walk along a hedgerow or in a field—to play a game of "I Spy"—to find a dandelion, and then another—to pick a bluebell and smell a wild rose. From earliest days they can be taught to revive in hot water their treasured wilting bunches of hedgerow pickings, and then to arrange them to enliven their precious Teddy Bears picnic; to present their offerings at the Christmas Crib; to plant their spring collection in the garden at Easter. Why not help them to collect the materials to make a moss and lichen garden? They will need a large flat plate or plastic tray or tin lid which will hold water. In this is arranged a selection (as large as possible) of different mosses, algae, selaginella and lichens, with perhaps some miniature ferns and tiny, favourite leaves. If kept continuously damp, the garden will last for many months on the window sill (but not in too-bright sunlight).

Among the endless lovely children's books and piles of favourite comics, why not include a colourful book on wild flowers and trees, a junior botany, a book on wild life? A drawing or painting book could be the start of a wild flower album, suitably labelled with the names of each harvesting—and why not a pressing book too, made of sheets of blotting paper?

Surely Margaret Rhodes, in her *Prayer for a Grandchild* which is quoted and illustrated on the facing page—as a message from me to Camilla—has the right idea?

147

SOME HERBALISTS

Take of the juice of mercurial eight pounds, of the juice of Burridg two pounds, of the juice of Buglosse two pounds. Mingle these with twelve pounds of clarrified Honey the whitest you can gett, let them boyle together aboyling and pass them through a Hypocras Bag of new flannell. Infuse in three pints of White Wine, a quarter of a pound Gentian Root and half a pound of Irish root or blew Flower de Lis. Let them be infused twenty fower houers then straind without squeezing, put the liquor to that of the herbs and Hony, boyle them well together to the consistance of a surrup. You must order the matter so that one thing stays not for the other but that all be ready together. A spoonfull of this surrup is to be taken every morning Fasting.

A receipt for the Surrup of Long Life to be done in the Moone of May—
Dr Peter Dumoulin   Thomas Newington
A Butler's Recipe Book, 1719

Pedanius Dioscorides——fl. c. A.D.50

Pedanius Dioscorides was born in Cilicia in the first century A.D. He is believed to have studied at Tarsus and at Alexandria, and then to have become a military physician with the Roman forces in Asia. His *De Materia Medica* is one of the earliest known herbals. He completed it in about A.D. 77, and it was still in use sixteen hundred years after his death.

Dioscorides names about five hundred different plants, many of which can no longer be identified. Under the name of each he gives a description of the plant, including its place of origin and usual habitat, with details of its uses in the preparation of drugs. A great many manuscripts of *De Materia Medica* exist. In the earlier versions an attempt is made at arranging the plants, but this does not go far enough to be called a system. In some of the later manuscripts an alphabetical arrangement is adopted.

Dioscorides is regarded as one of the founders of the science of Botany.

Alexander Neckam —— 1157–1217

Alexander Neckam was born in 1157 at St. Alban's in Hertfordshire. His mother was chosen as foster-mother to the Plantagenet baby Prince Richard, later Richard the Lion Heart, so that he and the future king were foster-brothers. Alexander became a scholar, and taught for some years at the University of Paris. He returned to England in 1186 and took up a post he had held earlier in his career, in charge of the school at Dunstable. He entered the Augustinian Order and rose to be Abbot of Cirencester in 1213. It was at about this time that he wrote *De Laudibus Divinæ Sapientes*, a verse re-writing of his earlier work *De Naturis Rerum*. *De Laudibus* is divided into ten parts, one of which is devoted to herbs. Neckam seems to have had a monkish interest in herbs and growing plants, but very little experience of the practical down-to-earth side of cultivation, or of properly scholarly botanical observation. He died in Worcestershire in 1217.

William Turner —— c. 1508–1568

William Turner was born at Morpeth in Northumberland in about 1508 and educated at Cambridge, where he studied medicine. He later took Holy Orders and became a convinced Protestant, so devoted to the Reformed religion that in 1540, during the reign of Henry VIII, he was forced to leave England. He travelled in Europe for the next four years, studying Botany in Ferrara and in Bologna. In 1547, following King Henry's death and the accession of the boy-King Edward VI, he returned to England. The Reformers were then firmly in power, one of their adherents being the Duke of Somerset, who was King Edward's uncle and Lord Protector of the Realm. William Turner prospered. He became Physician to the Lord Protector, and in 1550, Dean of Wells. But three years later the young King died; Mary Tudor, devoutly Catholic, was crowned Queen of England; and Turner was away on his travels again. He spent the next eight years living in Germany. Mary Tudor died in 1558 and was succeeded by her sister, Elizabeth; the Anglican religion was gradually established; and Turner was allowed to return to England, and was even reinstated as Dean of Wells once more. He was now in his fifties, however, and shortly decided to retire.

Turner's first botanical book was *Libellus De Re Herbaria*, published in 1538, before his first exile. This is a Latin catalogue of plant names, which also gives equivalent names in Greek and English. His *Names of Herbes* is a similar work and is a more extensive list in English, with German and French names added. These two books contain many of the first English records of plants growing in this country. They were based on his own original research. But his best-known work is his *Herball*, the first ever written in English, and the first English herbal to include original material. His interests seem to have leaned heavily towards the medical rather than the decorative, or delightful, qualities of herbs. The first part of *A Neue Herball* was brought out in 1551, the second in 1562; and the complete work was issued in 1568, the year of his death. In addition to his botanical work he wrote—inevitably—theological tracts; but also, with an engaging and admirable sixteenth century roundness, a book on birds (*Avium Precipuarum,*

1544), a work on fishes, another on mineral baths, and a third on the wines of England.

His attempts to classify and identify the flora of his time, both garden-grown and wild, earned him, deservedly, the nickname "Father of English Botany".

John Gerard —— 1545–1612

> To the large and singular furniture of this noble Island I have added from forreine places
> all varieties of herbs and flowers.that I might any way obtaine, I have laboured with the
> soile to make it fit for plants that they might delight in the soile.
>
> John Gerard: Dedication from the *Herball*

John Gerard was born in Cheshire in 1545. In his youth he travelled widely in Russia, Scandinavia, and the Mediterranean countries—possibly as a ship's doctor—but in his early thirties he returned to London and there settled down to the study of plants—in particular, plants with medicinal qualities—and took up a post as superintendent of Lord Burghley's garden. Burghley was Queen Elizabeth's trusted and chief counsellor, Lord Treasurer of England, a man who spent forty years dealing with weighty affairs of state, yet "after Bookes", a contemporary wrote of him, "his Garden was his chief pleasure." It was a garden full of his beloved gillyflowers. Gerard also cultivated a sizeable garden of his own in Holborn—"the little plot of myne own especiall care and husbandry"—which he catalogued in 1596, when it held over a thousand different plants. This is the earliest such catalogue of any single English garden, and of great importance to the botanical historian.

Gerard's famous *Herball* came out in 1597. It lists a host of English plants and is illustrated with 1,800 wood-cuts, each showing an entire plant—root, stem, flower and seed. Gerard gives the botanical name of each plant, its common name, the time of planting, the type of soil, the origin, "temperature", "virtues" and "use". He dedicated the *Herball* to Burghley, with a long and charming dedicatory notice.

Although the *Herball* was not original, being derived from the work of the Dutchman Dodoen, it remains a delightful and important survey of botanical knowledge at the end of the sixteenth century, and characteristically Elizabethan in its bold, enthusiastic determination to get everything in.

John Parkinson —— 1567–1650

John Parkinson was born in 1567. He is known to have been practising as an apothecary before 1616, and had a garden in Long Acre, in London, which was "well stored with rarities". He must have been a skilled and trusted man for he was appointed Apothecary to James I, and later, after James's death, King's Botanist to Charles I, his son. Among his acquaintances was another London apothecary, Thomas Johnson, who in 1636 rushed out a much-improved edition of Gerard's *Herball*, perhaps after hearing, on some apothecaries' grape-vine, that Parkinson was compiling his chief work, the elegant and decorative *Theatrum Botanicum or An Universall and Complete Herball*, which was eventually brought out in 1640. Like Bacon's earlier essay, *Of Gardens*, and many other seventeenth century writings, this work is full of appreciation of beauty and fragrance. One of Parkinson's earlier works, *Paradisi in Sole, Paradisus Terrestris* brought out in 1629 (its title being an appalling Latin pun on his own name: Park-in-sun), was the first English illustrated book devoted primarily to *ornamental* plants. It included sections on the kitchen garden and the orchard. He also compiled *Hortus Kewensis*. Thirty-three of the plants in the second edition are there recorded for the first time as growing in England. He died in 1650, but his name survives in *Parkinsonia*, a genus of Central American trees which was named in his honour.

Nicholas Culpeper——1616–1654

Nicholas Culpeper was born in 1616. He had a touching, resolute belief in the values of astrological medicine, and in 1640 established himself as a physician-astrologer in Spitalfields, London. In 1649 he fell out with the rest of the medical profession when he published, without authority, an English translation of the *Pharmacopœia* of the College of Physicians (they said acidly and incorrectly that he had put it into English "very filthily"). Four years later he produced *The English Physician Enlarged* which became immensely popular. He successfully combined a genuine faith in astrological herbalism with a deep devotion to the Puritan religion, and fought and was wounded in the Civil War. His early death in 1654 (leaving a widow and seven children) was said to have been caused by consumption, a consequence of his wound from which, apparently, no application of yarrow and other herbs, no horoscope-casting, no prayer could save him. His reputation, however, lived on (indeed Kipling describes him in *Rewards and Fairies*): a generous man, treating poor patients whether they could pay him or not, and holding fast to his convictions.

BIBLIOGRAPHY

Books

BAILEY, L. H. and Ethel Zoe, *Hortus Second*, The Macmillan Company, New York, 1941

BENTHAM, George, *Illustrated Handbook of the British Flora*, Lovell Reeve & Co., London, 1865

CHITTENDEN, F. J. *Dictionary of Gardening*, Oxford University Press, 1956

COATS, Alice M., *Flowers and their Histories*, Adam & Charles Black, London, 1968

———— *Garden Shrubs and their Histories*, Vista Books, London, 1963

COATS, Peter, *Flowers in History*, Weidenfeld & Nicholson, London, 1970

EMBERTON, Sybil, *Garden Foliage for Flower Arrangement*, Faber & Faber Ltd, London, 1968

EVERARD, Barbara and MORLEY, Brian, *Wild Flowers of the World*, Ebury Press & Michael Joseph Ltd, London, 1970

GRAVES, Robert, *The Greek Myths*, Penguin Books Ltd, London, 1955

HAY, Roy and SYNGE, Patrick M., *The Dictionary of Garden Plants*, Ebury Press & Michael Joseph Ltd, London, 1969

HELLYER, A. G. L., *Shrubs in Colour*, W. H. and L. Collingridge, London, 1965

KEBLE MARTIN, W., *The Concise British Flora in Colour*, Ebury Press & Michael Joseph Ltd, London, 1965

LEHNER, Ernst and Johanna, *Folklore and Symbolism of Flowers, Plants and Trees*, Tudor Publishing Company, New York, 1960

McCLINTOCK, David and FITTER, R. S. R., *Pocket Guide to Wild Flowers*, Collins (Wm.) Sons & Co Ltd, London, 1956

PICKSTON, Margaret, *The Language of Flowers*, Michael Joseph Ltd, London, 1968

SMITH, George W., *Flower Arrangements and their Setting*, Studio Vista Ltd, London, 1967

SPRY, Constance, *Anthology*, Dent (J. M.) & Sons Ltd, London, 1953

———— *Garden Notebook*, Dent (J. M.) & Sons Ltd, London, 1946

———— *How to Do the Flowers*, Dent (J. M.) & Sons Ltd, London, 1962

———— *Winter and Spring Flowers*, Dent (J. M.) & Sons Ltd, London, 1951

STEVENSON, Violet, *Dried Flowers for Decoration*, W. H. & L. Collingridge Ltd, London, and

Transatlantic Arts Inc., New York, 1955; revised edition, David and Charles (Publishers) Ltd, Newton Abbot, 1972

TERGIT, Gabriele, *Flowers Through the Ages*, Oswald Wolff, London, 1961

THOMAS, Graham S., *The Modern Florilegium*, Sunningdale Nurseries, 1957

UNDERWOOD, Mrs Desmond, *Grey and Silver Plants*, Collins (Wm.) Sons & Co Ltd, London, 1971

WHISTLER, Lawrence, *The English Festivals*, Heinemann (William) Ltd, London, 1947

Catalogues

Addresses (at the time of publication) are given on pages 154-155.

James CARTER & Co. (Seedsmen)

HILLIERS (Nurserymen and seedsmen)

Reginald KAYE Ltd (Nurserymen and fern specialists)

SUNNINGDALE Nurseries (Nurserymen)

SUTTON & Sons Ltd (Seedsmen)

THOMPSON & MORGAN (Seedsmen)

Mrs Desmond UNDERWOOD (Silver-foliaged plants)

WALLACE & BARR (Nurserymen and bulb specialists)

Herbals

Culpeper, Nicholas, *Complete Herbal*, Foulsham (W.) & Co Ltd, 1952

Dioscorides, Pedanius (ed. Gunther, R. T.) *Greek Herbal*, Hofner & Co Ltd, 1933

Gerard, John, (ed. Woodward, M.) *Herball*, Spring Books, 1964

Gerard's Herball, The Essence thereof, distilled by Marcus Woodward from the edition of Thomas Johnson, 1636, Minerva Press, reissued 1972

Periodicals

Amateur Gardening, Country Life, and *Popular Gardening* (all weekly), and *Homes and Gardens* (monthly), all from:

I.P.C. Magazines, Ltd, Kings Reach Tower, Stamford Street, London SE1 9LS.

Garden News (weekly):

E.M.A.P. National Publications Ltd, 21 Church Walk, Peterborough, Northants.

LIST OF ADDRESSES

Anjay Displays Ltd, 788 Harrow Road, London, N.W.10.
    — window and counter display-stand stockists.

James Carter & Co., Raynes Park, London, S.W.20.
    — seedsmen.

Robert Day & Co., Ltd, 4 Ladbroke Grove, London, W.11.
    — florist with special materials on sale.

Elaine Goddard Ltd, Discove, Bruton, Somerset.
    — flower vases.

Handley Reed & Co., 68 Mansey Street, London, SE17 1JP.
    — floral ware and accessories.

Harbutts Plasticine Ltd, Bathampton, Bath.
    — Plasticine and Plastone.

Henry (Florist), 4 Trinity Road, London, S.W.17.
    — florist.

Hilliers, 5 Street Mead, Bowden, Winchester, Hampshire.
    — nurserymen and seedsmen.

Reginald Kaye Ltd., Silverdale, Carnforth, Lancs.
    — nurserymen and fern specialists.

Natural Fern Display Centre, 73 Monmouth Street, London, W.C.2.
    — dried flower material.

Perry's Hardy Plant Farm, Enfield, Middlesex.
    — nurserymen.

Progressive Suppliers Paper Ltd, 18 Crawford Place, London W1H 2AJ.
    — Finoplas paper for wrapping delicate arrangements.

Pulbrooke & Gould, 181 Sloane Street, London, S.W.1.
— florists.

Constance Spry, 98 Marylebone Lane, London, W.1.
— floral specialists.

Stemfix Accessories Ltd, Magpie Lane, Sedgwick, Horsham, Sussex.
— Stemfix floral foam, Stemfix adhesive, preserving crystals, etc.

Sunningdale Nurseries, Windlesham, Surrey.
— nurserymen.

Sutton & Sons Ltd, Reading, Berkshire.
— seedsmen.

Thompson & Morgan Ltd, London Road, Ipswich, Suffolk.
— seedsmen.

Mrs Desmond Underwood, Ramparts Nurseries, Brainswick, Colchester, Essex.
— silver-foliaged plants.
— (following the sad death of Mrs Underwood, the Nurseries have remained open.)

Wallace & Barr Ltd, Marden, Kent.
— nurserymen and bulb specialists.

A PERSONAL GLOSSARY

of the Flower-Arranging Terms used in this book
with some transatlantic equivalents

an **all-round** arrangement is one which is circular and can be viewed from all sides.

the **basal front** ⎫ are terms for the focal point
the **central base** ⎭ of the arrangement.

the **central top** is the topmost point in height.

the **centrepiece** is another name for the focal point.

conditioning is a specialised treatment to prevent a flower from flagging or wilting and assist it to remain turgid; the term relates only to the liquid content of the plant.

a **cone-shaped** arrangement is usually assembled on a conical frame of wire netting, which is packed with damp Oasis and fitted onto a stand; sprigs of box or other evergreens can then be inserted through the wire mesh to give a clipped topiary effect, and decorated with baubles—for Christmas, perhaps—or small flower-heads (a beautiful cone-shaped arrangement is illustrated in *Flower Arrangements and Their Setting*, by George W. Smith).

glue: a North American alternative is "bond-fast".

glycerine treatment is a preserving method used for leaves; the transatlantic equivalent is "folia-cure".

grooming means cleaning, trimming and shaping material for use in an arrangement; the term is applied both to fresh and dried flower work.

gutta-percha: a transatlantic equivalent is "flora-tape".

infilling means filling in the gaps in an arrangement, as necessary; tucking in material to fill the spaces; an alternative term is "fill-in work".

insetting is recessed infilling.

outlining: the outer edges of an arrangement (both in height and width); the arrangement's silhouette.

pinholders are known as "needlepoint" holders across the Atlantic.

plastic adhesive: the North American equivalent is "stickem".

preserving crystals: the chemical crystals in which some flowers can be immersed for drying; crystals of silica gel are useful for this; the transatlantic equivalent is "flora-cure".

recessed: inset.

reel wire: otherwise known as spool wire.

sellotape: known across the Atlantic as "Scotch tape".

shadow leaves: skeletonised leaves, sold commercially.

skeletonising: a process whereby some forms of hard, glossy leaves can be immersed for several weeks in water and allowed to decompose. The green, fleshy tissues on the upper and under surfaces of the leaves will eventually rot away (or can be carefully removed) and the tougher leaf tissues will remain as a skeleton structure. This then has to be carefully washed and dried by pressing flat (holly leaves are an exception).

stub wire: a North American equivalent is "stem wire".

a **three-dimensional** arrangement is one in which the material is assembled in such a way that the combination of recessed material and projecting material, alternately lightening and condensing, creates a special effect—one can, as it were, see "through" the various layers. Fig. 19 on page 65 is an example of such an arrangement.

twist-its (plant ties): a similar transatlantic product is "twist-ems".

GLOSSARY OF BOTANICAL TERMS

annual: a plant that completes its life within one year, through germination and flowering and seeding to death. Gardeners, however, often use the word *annual* to mean a plant that blooms the first year from seed, whether or not it dies that same year.

anther: the male sexual organ which is the head of a flower's stamen, in which the pollen grains are formed; when ripe, the anther opens and expels the pollen

axil: the angle that lies between the stem and the petiole or peduncle

basal: leaves at the base of the plant

biennial: a plant that lives for two years from seed, flowering only (or mostly) in the year following sowing

botryoid: shaped like a bunch of grapes

bract (dim. **bracteole**): a much-modified leaf, especially a tiny leaf growing on the upper part of flowering stems or in a flower-cluster

calyx: the whorl, or outer circle, of sepals, which may be either separate or joined together at their outer edges to form, for example, a cup-shaped calyx. Its primary purpose is to protect the bud.

capitulum: a dense, compact cluster of florets congregated on a common platform

carpel: the female sexual organ, whose base is the ovary (containing the ovule which after pollination develops into the seed); one of the units of a compound pistil (a simple pistil being a single carpel)

conifer: a cone-bearing tree, such as the cypress

corolla: the circle, or whorl, of petals which grows within the calyx

crucifer: a member of the *Cruciferæ* (mustard) family, which have four-sepalled and four-petalled flowers, and are thus said to be cross-shaped

cultivar: a variety that has originated under cultivation and cannot necessarily be referred to a botanical species

deciduous: a tree that sheds its leaves yearly

double blooms: flowers that have more than the usual number of petals

evergreen: a tree which does not shed its leaves annually but remains green throughout the year

family: an association of genera (which may be vast, as in the case of the *Compositæ* family—towards 1,000—or, as in the case of *Punica*, may consist of one genus only) which resemble each other in general appearance and in technical character

filament: the stalk-like part of the stamen that supports the anther

florescence: the flowering or blossoming of a plant

floret: a tiny flower which with a mass of others makes up a dense inflorescence; one of the small individual flowers of a composite or grass

genus: a group of plants comprising one or more species, which are closely related and agree in one or more important structural character. About 10,000 genera are commonly recognised. The first of the two words in the botanical designation of a plant is its generic name.

glaucous: having a bluish-green "bloom" on its surface

hybrid: the product of a cross between two species (a **half-hybrid** is the product of a cross between one species and a variety of another species)

immortelle: frequently called an everlasting, this is a plant—often with a papery look or texture—which retains its form and colour when dried

inflorescence: a flower-cluster

involucre: a whorl of bracts growing close underneath a flower or flower-cluster

lateral: on or at the side

latifoliate: broad-leaved

leaflet: a small leaf; one of the parts of a compound leaf

lobe: a division of a leaf

node: the point at the juncture of leaf and stem

order: a group of genera, all agreeing in some striking particular

ovary: the closed chamber at the base of the pistil which contains the ovule

ovule: the body which, after fertilization, becomes the seed

palmate: shaped like the palm of the hand

panicle: a loose flower-cluster, supported on branched pedicels

pedicel: a flower-stalk supporting a flower in a cluster

perennial: a plant that survives for more than two years: larkspur, for example

petal: one of the leaves of a corolla

petiole: a leaf-stalk

pinnate: the elongated leaflets of a compound leaf placed in pairs on either side of an axis

pistil: the ovule-bearing body, comprising the ovary, stigma, and style

pollen: the fertilizing powder expelled by the anther, which fertilizes the ovule

raceme: a simple elongated cluster of flowers borne on footstalks

radical leaves: those which spring from the root, i.e. basal

scape: a leafless flower-stalk rising direct from the rootstock; a tulip, for instance, is borne on a scape

sepal: a leaf of the calyx

species: a group of plants which have marked

or essential characters in common. Species are combined into genera. The name of a species consists of two words, the first representing the genus and the second identifying the particular kind or member of the genus

spike: a compact elongated cluster of flowers without footstalks

stamen: the male pollen-bearing organ, consisting of the anther and the filament

stigma: the part of the pistil (usually at the top of the pistil) that receives the pollen grains

style: the support for the stigma

terminal: produced at the summit of the stem

trefoil: a leaf composed of three leaflets, the clover being one of the most common examples

umbel: a flat-topped cluster of flowers whose footstalks are approximately equal in length, radiating outwards from a single point

umbellifer: belonging to the genus of *Umbelliferæ*; umbels are characteristic of the *Umbelliferæ*

variegated: marked with different patches of colour

variety: a subordinate class of plants within a species. There are two ranges of varieties: the first display fairly marked differences in nature, and thus are dignified with a Latin botanical name (*Sambucus canadensis* var. *aurea*, for example); the second display small or artificial differences and are given vernacular names

whorl: a ring of leaves or flowers round a stem

INDEX

by S. A. Manning